ACCELERATED LEARNING

By Leon Lyons

About the Author

Leon Lyons is a senior coach at Mindset Mastership, a life coaching business based in London, England. Mindset Mastership teaches clients how human behavior really works. Through our teaching we have helped worldwide clients gain a better advantage, to develop themselves and achieve more from life.

WANT A COPY OF MY NEW EBOOK?

Email me:

MindsetMastership@gmail.com

© **Copyright 2021 by (United Arts Publishing, England.)
- All rights reserved.**

This document is geared towards providing exact and reliable information in regards to the topic and issue covered. The publication is sold with the idea that the publisher is not required to render accounting, officially permitted, or otherwise, qualified services. If advice is necessary, legal or professional, a practised individual in the profession should be ordered.

- From a Declaration of Principles which was accepted and approved equally by a Committee of the American Bar Association and a Committee of Publishers and Associations.

In no way is it legal to reproduce, duplicate, or transmit any part of this document in either electronic means or in printed format. Recording of this publication is strictly prohibited and any storage of this document is not allowed unless with written permission from the publisher. All rights reserved.

The information provided herein is stated to be truthful and consistent, in that any liability, in terms of inattention or otherwise, by any usage or abuse of any policies, processes, or directions contained within is the solitary and utter responsibility of the recipient reader. Under no circumstances will any legal responsibility or blame be held against the publisher for any reparation, damages, or monetary loss due to the information herein, either directly or indirectly.

Respective authors own all copyrights not held by the publisher.

The information herein is offered for informational purposes solely, and is universal as so. The presentation of the information is without contract or any type of guarantee assurance.

The trademarks that are used are without any consent, and the publication of the trademark is without permission or backing by the trademark owner. All trademarks and brands within this book are for clarifying purposes only and are the owned by the owners themselves, not affiliated with this document.

Table of Contents

Introduction 1

Chapter 1: Learn With Mind Maps 7

Chapter 2: Speed Reading 20

Chapter 3: Memory Improvement 32

Chapter 4: NLP Tips & Techniques For Faster Learning 51

Chapter 5: Boosting Your IQ 62

Chapter 6: Boosting Your Ability To Learn 75

Chapter 7: Develop Massive Self-Confidence And Self-Esteem 88

Chapter 8: Retention And Comprehension Skill 100

Chapter 9: Develop A Photographic Memory And Improvement .. 112

Chapter 10: Skills To Remember Quicker 124

Chapter 11: Increase Memory Productivity 137

Chapter 12: Feedback And Iteration 150

Conclusion 166

References 168

Join Our

Personal Growth Power Group

To help reinforce the learning's from our books, I strongly suggest you join our well-informed powerhouse community on Facebook.

Here, you will connect and share with other like-minded people to support your journey and help you grow.

>>>Click here to join Our Personal Growth Support Group <<<

Introduction

Learning, A Continual Process

The purpose of the book is to provide you with the best ways to cut poor learning habits and to enhance your brain to a level that it becomes hard to simply forget anything.

Learning is not only recognizing the answers to questions or situations. It's not simply the acquisition of basic knowledge bits and pieces. Scores and examination results can't really calculate it. It's simply not taking what other individuals know on board.

Learning is a continual process. To develop your own individual conception, it's an endless journey of adventure. And it ought to include the capacity to continually evaluate and enhance the manner in which you learn—the capacity to be aware of the system of your personal thinking and learning. Learning has to start long before the first day of school for the kid and ought to continue even into retirement.

We should never cease learning and putting into practice whatever we have learned. What consequences are there? We desperately have to implement changes.

In nearly every profession, knowledge doubles every three or four years, and this implies that the knowledge should double each three to four years just in order to remain even. Individuals that do not upgrade their knowledge and learning skills actively and consistently do not remain in the same position. They just fail to keep up with others.

Where do you decide to be, you ought to ask yourself this question? Consider the disappearance of your sector. What will be your next step in your professional life? What qualities do you possess that you can leverage on? What do you have to be exceptional at? Are you ready to cope with the face-paced modern world? After all, change is just another term for development, a different synonym for learning. When we wish to, we can all try it and love it,' says British futurist Professor Charles Handy, past president of the Royal Society for the Encouragement of Arts, Manufactures, and Commerce (RSA).

These were previously skills required by just a few "great executives." We simply need them for survival nowadays. Everybody wants to concentrate quality thinking on what he wants to know to do great in his career, for both tomorrow and today.

The biggest distinction between individuals in our community was among people who "have more" and the people who "have less." Nowadays, instead, the distinction is between people who "know more" and the people who "know less," says Brian Tracy, author of Maximum Achievement and one of the biggest skilled trainers and workshop leaders in America.

The Mind, A Powerful Learning Tool

You are a massive computer for learning. At this time, however you think towards developing new skills and topics, know that your memory and system have developed over thousands of years to be the earth's most powerful ability and information development tool. It's a basic fact.

However, without a guide, as the case with any computer or super electronic, we do not have the idea of how to utilize it to its maximum potential appropriately. For the human brain and system, it's exactly the same. We are yet to make an effective application of our ability to learn for the majority of human existence. We really had no idea of how. For the students in classrooms, regrettably, the manner in which things are learned produces detrimental emotions related to discovering new comprehension or reading skills in several of us—at the same time superimposing in our minds peculiar and counterproductive methods for learning. Typically, the school system is centered on an obsolete approach that was established over a hundred years ago. At the time, people have far less knowledge about how the human brain functions and learns.

The least appealing part of it, we also establish prejudices at school that we may not be able to learn those things, as well as other garbage of that sort. It's important to abandon them and embrace the transformative reality if you have struggled with convictions like these. You can learn and understand whatever you want, and even quicker than you expect.

Need for Accelerated Learning

You may well not accept it, but you're twice as clever as you feel you really are! The basic guides inside this piece will illustrate this to you by; increasing your reading and learning rate, your ability to master any technique or topic and address issues, and your willingness to think things out fast when you need to!

Your continued success will rely on your capacity to learn information, techniques, and methods and bring them to practical application in this modern, rapidly-changing world of ours! Allow me to reiterate that, regardless of how old you are, male or a female, self-employed or employed in a big company, your capacity to read, learn, to make your brain function effectively will decide the whole quality of your life.

I mean, the volume of your salary, the destination you enter in life, the type of individual who will select you as his mate, even the enjoyment you derive out of your leisure time hobbies, everything will be determined by your capacity to keep pace with and, if necessary, advance forward with hundreds of thousands of people who compete with you.

About This Book

This book will modify your brain if you have initially doubted your learning skills. e You will become an extremely successful learner by applying the content of this book. Your brain is, without a doubt, a supercomputer. The details offered in this book will enable you to activate your mind's incredible ability.

This book is written in a concise, and engaging tone, instead of the academic tone which often turn off a readers attention. This was carried out deliberately. Even if I was a devoted and committed student, I frequently struggled to read academic books due to their extremely dry presentation. I wouldn't like that to be the case with this piece. The details provided in this book can practically transform your life, and I like to ensure you study it all!

My aim is for you to genuinely derive pleasure reading this book. On a Weekend night, you also might discover yourself sitting home as you simply can't drop it. Okay, I concede that may be a little improbable, but I hope you're having a good time learning how best to learn.

You're going to be fitted with different approaches to help your life transform from repetitious and unconcerned to thrilling and alert.

You would be shown through verified methods how to improve your memory and your ability to read with speed, particularly with respect to scholars and routine life in general. As a result of your irritating practice of forgetting stuff that counts, you no more have to think about the disaster you end up making. Your career will be guided towards a significant shift in a simple language after you have read this book.

Now let start our voyage of accelerated learning, with no further delay!

Chapter 1:
Learn With Mind Maps

Meaning of Mind Mapping?

You've read a lot about mind mapping; however, you don't understand why mind maps are completely awesome to apply in your daily life. They are capable of improving our memory, enable us to learn, encourage us to better remember books, and really just begin to enhance each area of our lives.

Firstly, let us go over just what a mind map is, and later we'll go over the way you can make your life easier by using one. It can be achieved whether by hand or by applying software; however, the main objective is to draw out a core idea or concept creatively.

Without recognizing we were doing it, most of us have at one point used mind maps in a certain form or fashion. You've encountered a mind map if you've once been in a classroom or seminar in which the individual leading it illustrated a core concept on the board and then linked related ideas to it with lines.

It was most probably a really simple sort, but nevertheless, it was one. For years, Mind maps have existed and were born out of other related ideas that have been around for a far longer time. Simply, mind mapping is whenever a diagram discusses a concept, phrase, or theory.

For instance, perhaps somebody wishes to go over and explore a book they just read. They will place the title of the book at the core of the mind map, and then the supporting ideas and concepts are placed with lines, circles, squares, pictures, or patterns. The application of color and some other innovative uses of the different pieces used in the mind map emphasizes details.

How to Construct a Simple Mind Map

Mind maps are quite simple to build. The power of mind maps lies in using them. So I'm going to send you the guidelines you'd follow to make a simple mind map whenever you begin with mind maps and working out the way to most effectively use them. You might apply a few mind mapping free software if you are really tech-savvy and can handle innovative ideas when learning new software. But if you want to place your pen on paper, you may make a chart of your mind by hand. There are a few small ways to bear in mind, irrespective of the way you produce the mind map.

- Begin with a central idea.

You would like to ensure that you get a solid idea with the mind map that you can examine. Make sure the definition is large enough to sketch out the mind map in a useful manner. You would like to ensure that the idea is specific enough not to make you end up with numerous mind maps. You like to delve into one subject and go as far as you are able to without another subject muddying it.

- Note down the various concepts relating to the idea.

Write down the terms that spring to mind as they refer to the core idea. With the aid of lines, connect certain terms to the core concept and highlight the words. Using single words and keeping the words down to the lowest minimum. Apply upper and lower case alphabets to highlight particular points. Many mind maps are usually about key terms; therefore they make the most of certain key terms, not phrases or clauses. There are several exceptions to this rule, but I will concentrate on key terms.

- Using pictures and symbols instead of words

Using pictures and symbols rather than words wherever necessary. It's cool if you're not drawing. Quite clear stick figure pictures or plain symbols may be used. The idea is for you to incorporate a visual aspect to the mind map to convey a message.

- Using shapes to categorize words or picture sets

Anytime you build a word or picture collection, you may use shapes to represent a connection among them. For instance, you might place the whole of the words and images in circles if you're handling a particular area of the central subject. Then you may place all of the words and images in rectangles if you're handling another field. You might apply less traditional shapes like cones if you feel adventurous, though the primary objective is to offer a fantastic look to our mind map.

- To show relationships, add colors

It's essential that in our mind map, we use various colors. You can apply at least three different colors; however, look for methods to use more. In addition to using shapes in mind maps, signs, and pictures, colors can be used instead. In the use of colour, be imaginative.

You're on the journey to building a simple mind map when you've taken these steps into action. This will offer you the chance to get more relaxed utilizing mind maps in the most realistic manner. The most vital thing to note is that you're not simply making a beautiful picture. You are constructing a visual sample of the way information is interpreted by your mind as it applies to the core principle.

Mind Mapping Your Day

We live busy lives. Our lives are not solely loaded with routine tasks such as working and attending school. They are equally filled with a lot more things than it has ever been. 1 in 3 working individuals work more than 48 hours a week, leaving little time for other everyday tasks such as fitness, recreation, chores, and other items that might occur during the day. Mind maps can be applied to coordinate our everyday tasks, and there are advantages to doing so.

- Better recall of everyday duties

How much do you return home from office work only to find that you failed to do anything on the way home that you really wanted to do? Even when you are careful in preparing a to-do list, such lists can also appear to go on indefinitely, and you may miss stuff. Mind maps are designed to allow you to see anything on it right at a glimpse. You would be better able to remember them whenever appropriate by using colors to illustrate the most vital items on your list in conjunction with relevant key terms.

- Rapid prioritization of duties

It's simple to get irritated whenever you're looking at a long list, especially when you have so many tasks to handle at a given time. Since you may apply colors and lines inside a mind map to illustrate various activities, it is possible to assess priority based on whatever is most urgent. You can take a look at the mind map and check what's most essential and work on those assignments first.

- Introduce new behaviours

Three items that each one wants to focus on doing better and more always are eating more nutritious food, exercising, and having more rest. By planning it in our day and emphasizing the advantages of doing so, you may employ a mind map to enable you to build new behaviours. You can also develop a schedule whereby you arrange incentives for particular targets to be accomplished.

- Enhanced productivity

In order to maximize general productivity, task lists are fine. However, mind maps could be even better. One of the drawbacks of task lists is that they are mostly prepared using long sentences or expressions. This may make it difficult to properly handle them, particularly when you have so many tasks to achieve. And who didn't have a task list that was longer than a page? Since mind maps apply key terms and connections, it is intended to tap into our memory efficiently. Also, having the capacity to observe all of our roles in one visually appealing schedule makes it simpler to examine all of them in a significant way.

Mind Maps for Studying and Taking Notes

It's not simple to go to school. In particular, it's not supposed to be easy if you're studying for a degree. You also juggle various classes on numerous subjects that need the same amount of focus and concentration. The knowledge needed to succeed in our classrooms can be difficult to obtain and process efficiently. In streamlining the note-taking procedure in class and the study process after classroom lessons, Mind maps can be quite effective.

Have you ever skipped anything meaningful when you were attempting to put down something that the teacher or professor just described?

The long hand could be distracting to take notes, and not so many people do great with using a short hand. Nevertheless, you will be able to easily obtain and jot down information if you start using mind maps while taking notes.

Integrating Mind Maps When Taking Notes or Studying

- Enhances Comprehension

Although it can take a little time getting acquainted with writing notes with a mind map, once you start taping into the various way our mind functions and the manner to express that on paper, you'll see yourself interpreting knowledge far more efficiently. Since mind maps combine in group and word association, they immediately allow the maker of the map to use present knowledge to connect to the latest information obtained. One of the strategies to enhance memory and knowledge gathering is by associating and grouping new knowledge with old ones. Mind maps inherently promote that sort of thought, which implies that fresh knowledge is much faster understood and more efficient.

- Enhances note-taking pace

Anytime you make long-hand notes, you need to reflect on the things the instructor or speaker is saying to concentrate on the note you are taking.

This may make you miss the transfer of vital details while you are writing. It may be really difficult taking notes this manner, which is why some folks begin recording lectures and discussions, gathering many important details? Although this is one approach to solving the question, it can come with its own collection of challenges, doing double as much work as in note-taking.

When you get home and ready to review the details, you need to transcribe the audio file or go over it and listen to it several times to take notes. It can be hard to do if you are taking several courses or just have a limited period of time to prepare. Mind maps will cut all of that out without losing knowledge gain. You can easily take into account what is exchanged and arrange it in a manner that is important to you by using key terms, shapes, and colours. You will come back to it later this way and understand what you meant to observe.

- Organizes your ideas

The individual speaking will also share many details and phrases while you're listening in a lecture room or a class, though not all of it can be jotted down or recalled. Much of what is discussed is to describe or connect particular concepts to the class. In sketches or lists, there are several individuals who talk and explicitly state the issue to be addressed prior to discussing it. These individuals make taking notes from their lectures very convenient. Sadly, these individuals are not really popular, and you're going to find yourself listening to even less straightforward talks or lectures.

It is essential to be able to discern whatever you have to know from what's simply supportive discussion. If you get a lot of details in this manner, it can be hard to structure our opinions accordingly. Mind maps are outstanding at enabling you to arrange the knowledge you gather so that at the moment, you can hold it and analyze it later.

I understand that with classes and learning, sometimes the details you require is in a journal. Yes, mind maps are excellent for orally gathering knowledge, but it is equally a good way to learn written content.

Mind Maps for Writing and Reading

Much of the mind map strategies addressed were related to analyzing data or organizing something. To assist with reading as well as writing anything from scratch, mind maps may equally be helpful. Several individuals utilize outlines to plan to write or just jump in and start to write. The same applies to reading. Until you begin reading something, many of you don't do any planning work. We're just going to begin reading and then go from there. Mind maps, however, can be excellent resources to render us better writers and productive readers.

Mind Maps to Read

You can apply a mind map to arrange the details as you are on the verge of undertaking a reading assignment that requires a lot of complicated information or several details that you need to keep for later use. Below are several steps to take when reading to ensure the most use of a mind map.

- Begin the mind map in the middle with the title of the book. This would be a mind map of the whole book and will most definitely cover many subjects as you scan through the pages of the book. Therefore it's good, to begin with, the title of the book over a central concept or subject.

- Build actual linkages to the key subjects mentioned in the book or book sections. Before you begin reading the book, make it as simple as possible and ensure you do this.
- Go over and put down whatever questions you think about in every section of the book chapter. You would like to discuss the questions you have ahead so that you can check for those answers when reading. Only by putting them down and remembering them, you would be able to see the replies even though you are not actively looking for them.
- Begin Reading. You'll be able to begin reading the book when you've begun with your mind map. The key advice is never to try to be aware of the map when reading. Concentrate on reading the content in huge pieces, then return back and map it by the time you're finished. Try to read up an entire chapter by the time you begin, then mind map the chapter. Cut down the size of the piece you read if this is difficult for you. As you become used to mind mapping, you could always develop it. You will find that you remember the things you read by the time you begin this phase, and you are able to view them much faster later.

Mind Maps for Writing

As they plan to compose something, some authors are meticulous in making outlines. To start with, this is a fantastic habit, though it doesn't usually work for everybody. However before, you begin to write. It does enable you to have some sort of action plan. Mind maps may appeal to some more individuals in a fashion that outlines do not encourage the creative process. It is fair that mind maps will function effectively for books that are so science-oriented as they assist with gathering facts, reports, and findings, but they can equally work for fiction books.

To derive the most of a mind map for writing, below are some measures to adopt.

- Begin the mind map with your key theme for the book. Concentrate on the book's overall purpose and create space for things to alter when you begin preparing. Don't make it too precise that your mind map appears as a planning trap.
- Ascertain the most significant component of the book and build sections to represent that. For instance, if your chunk of writing is quite character-oriented, then the characters would be centered on your first category of sections. If your chunk of writing has to discuss particular subjects, those sections will be those subjects.

- Widen the sections depending on the way you perceive each one evolving as the book is published. This is the area you will plan the way you like to advance the book or illustrate various aspects of the subjects you like to discuss. This is not set in stone but offers a fantastic structure to get you on course to touch on anything you like in the book.
- Start writing your book. Applying a mind map to write can certainly render writing even more efficient in a manner that helps to optimize the creative process. Sadly, outlines may often feel like dealing with more, which is the reason people don't use them. My purpose is not to prevent the use of outlines but to offer you an alternative way. Please do so if you like to proceed with using your outlines. Although if you wish to attempt something new, you may include mind maps in your writing tools. You would surely have an enhanced writing experience by using a planning process that gets the creative juices flowing when arranging and structuring your ideas.

Chapter 2:
Speed Reading

The Basic Concept of Speed Reading

It is crucial that you realize what speed reading is really all about prior to learning the tactics and approaches that will help you be a skilled speed reader. Speed reading is a style of reading that aims to absorb the most relevant knowledge without being deterred by the word by word descriptions of a specific text or piece of written content, unlike thorough reading or active reading. Speed reading, similar to the skimming reading method, would therefore allow you to distinguish significant details without needing to take the time and energy to read the entire word in the text.

Also, you will have the capacity to read the words you have to more quickly and clearly than the types of reading you are already using. Consequently, you will be prepared to do so in as little as half of the time you will need in your present reading pace, even if you have to do the more tedious reading.

The basic thing about speed reading to realize is that it seeks to return the quality and convenience of reading that pictorial languages offered to the people several years ago. The benefit of pictorial representation, as mentioned previously, is that they include complete meanings in simple signs and images, which modern languages are generally incapable of doing.

"Speed reading is the reading technique that allows you to overlook the endless amount of characters that have little or no intrinsic value."

If you avoid noticing the number of words per paragraph you read essentially contain useful information, you will find that quarter or more of the words applied is wholly redundant. This suggests that about half of the period you spend reading is expended on blank or unfamiliar words, words that actually do not earn the time it requires to read them. Although it can take considerable training to get very efficient at being able to figure out the words that count in sentences, the truth is that immediately you understand how to read beyond the irrelevant words and highly concentrate on the words that have meanings, you will quickly start to increase your pace.

The next idea that is important to consider about speed reading is that it eliminates reading's analytical aspect. We are able to read a written text all too quickly with a discerning lens, one that identifies spelling or grammatical mistakes. Needless to say, with such a discerning lens, the amount of time and the energy it requires to read anything is much more than sufficient. The odds are that the item you are reading is not really graded, so there is no point to objectively evaluate the way it is written. This is an important explanation why reading every single word with the same attention is unintuitive to the entire purpose of reading, which is to obtain a basic impression or concept via written words. By reading with the sole goal of seeing the image found in the words, you would have the ability to decrease the amount of time it requires you to read each text by an entire two-thirds of your present pace.

Finally, it is necessary to remember the key purpose of speed reading. Most individuals have been taught to learn by speaking out loudly. This was a very important move because it made it easier for a teacher to determine whether a student was finding difficulty with any specific element of reading. Essentially, reading aloud was more for the instructor's good than those of the student himself. Ultimately, students were advised to avoid reading aloud until the teacher was sure that they might read effectively. Sadly, what persisted was a voice saying each and every single phrase in the reader's mind as it was read. As pronouncing words requires time, the general reading acceleration of an average individual is drastically decreased. Therefore, what destroys the average individual's reading pace is the idea that they put in the effort to say the words when they read them in their head, an approach that is a horrific waste of time and effort.

Speed reading allows an individual to eliminate that part, opening their brain to hold more details and allowing them to read every text a minimum of two times quickly by not saying every word in their minds.

Speed reading, ultimately, is not just all about enabling you to read the exact words in much lesser time. Instead, speed reading is all about motivating you to fully rethink the manner in which you read. You will start to consider the written text as a body of knowledge that needs just visual comprehension, rather than assuming the written text as the spoken word spelled out. Therefore, you will start to read paragraphs very much like images read by the ancient people, visualizing the details instead of the writing process itself. All the times you have vast portions of the document to read to gather valuable knowledge will greatly help. Speed reading will enable you to decrease the text down to the essential components alone whilst enabling you to read the information with speed and intent simultaneously, decreasing the time and energy taken to read each item significantly.

What to Gain from Speed Reading

The word 'speed reading' demonstrates the main purpose of the provided techniques and tactics to enhance the speed at which an individual read. This alone would be important to anyone, but the fact is that skilled speed readers get much more than simply the prowess to read faster. The brain will act as a kind of sponge, consuming what it sees and hears.

As the average reader spends his time and energy reading every text that is written, this implies that the brain of the ordinary individual seeks to suck up each text they read when saying such words in their head. This causes a terrible instance of the overwhelming amount of information, where even the brain is desperately working to interpret each and every term that the actual meaning of the writing can often be confused.

Consequently, when an individual employs the speed reading approach to read through the texts and get straight to the core of the presented content, they are able to hold much more details because their brain is not clouded with the job of interpreting every single term. Therefore, speed reading will not solely improve an individual's reading speed. It will equally increase their general understanding of reading, rendering them to be a more successful reader at all stages.

Although it can require as little as 24 hours or less to master the art of speed reading, the further you keep practicing speed reading, the better it will help you. You'll improve your memory greatly as you build the strategies for effective speed reading. This is due to the fact that you will start to read for the purpose of getting knowledge, instead of merely for the purpose of reading. Therefore, as you put in the effort to read more and more rapidly, your brain will adapt in a manner that will allow you to interpret information more rapidly and hold it for extended periods. This is something that will yield huge benefits in the long run, whether you are reading for the purpose of your job, education, or just for fun. Now, not only are you going to be able to read quicker, you will also be able to read smarter.

Tools Required for Speed Reading

When you have built the proper setting, the proper time, and the proper attitude for your voyage into the realm of speed reading, you have to ensure you acquire all the necessary resources needed for the voyage. Such tools, most of which you may already have, are mainly simple pieces. In fact, even when you don't have an actual tool suggested, it's probably you'll be able to replace it with another thing you already have. This implies that in 24 hours or less, with no extra cost or inconvenience, you ought to be able to accomplish your target of enhancing your reading speed and reading ability.

A good watchmaker is the first item that you would require. Most speed reading services suggest that you acquire a stopwatch since this is the perfect manner of recording the duration a specific passage took you to read. It is quite useful to have a stopwatch or a monitor with a reminder for most workouts, as this helps you to concentrate entirely on reading without needing to keep a close watch on the time. Often, do not worry if you cannot get a stopwatch or an alarm timer.

There's a possible chance that you have, and you just don't know it! In your kitchen, look around and see whether you have an egg timer or anything close.

A pointer is also a tool you will require. Luckily, this can appear in any kind of shape or size. For activities involving a pointer, applying a pen, a pencil, or maybe your finger would probably be enough. The main idea is to locate an object that is easy to carry, and that doesn't overtly draw your attention. You'll like to keep a record of your development as you improve your speed reading skill. It is strongly advisable to have a little journal reserved for your speed reading activities. This gives you a spot to log your time for reading and material to put down the responses to your activities' queries.

There'll be instances where you have to evaluate your reading comprehension, so you would like to put down your responses in such situations. In addition, keeping a journal would offer you material to put down any particular questions, objectives, or thoughts you have developed along the way. Again, this is a kind of voyage and every individual experience this voyage in a different manner. So, It is quite necessary that this voyage be tailored in all possible ways. Identify your objectives, barriers, and other metrics that will enable you to accomplish your ultimate goal.

Strategies for Efficient Speed Reading

Speed reading can be easily divided into different fundamental concepts:

- Non-vocalization
- Enhanced reading speed
- Grouping of words
- and lastly, skimming.

These four principles can enable you to deal with the capacity to interpret from all directions. Consequently, you would not solely acquire fresh skills but also cut off the bad practices that limit your reading speed and your understanding of reading more often than not. You would improve the number of words you read every minute by adopting this method, the volume of reading you may do in just a sitting, and eventually, the pace at which you acquire information from every written document. These abilities will allow you to be a more skilled and productive reader, giving you the full outcomes from the amount of time and energy you put into reading.

Nonvocalization

The first approach for mastering speed reading is non-vocalization. Only when you can see a word without really pronouncing it in your mind would you be able to free yourself from the slow reading pace you are used to. Typically, this is the biggest obstacle, and so it is the first to be tackled.

The other speed reading techniques are focused on your capacity to read content without articulating the text. Therefore it is crucial to accomplish non-vocalization as swiftly as possible. Pointless to mention, as this is the toughest obstacle for everyone to solve, it will take a reasonable amount of training until you are completely free from this negative habit.

Please ensure you spend as much time as possible to master this ability. You would only have the capacity to raise your reading speed to some significant level if you can read without saying the words in your head.

Enhanced reading speed

The next technique for mastering speed reading is to raise the number of words you read every minute. This is more like attempting, in a manner, to reduce the period it requires to run a mile distance. They also evaluate running times anytime you encounter runners speaking. Although some claim that they can run an eight-minute mile, others might claim that they can do the same in just six minutes or even less. The basis of how competent an individual is at racing is the minutes per mile scale. Reading is almost the same.

Grouping

Another immensely useful approach is word grouping to maximize the average word per minute count. This approach concentrates on reading collections of words instead of a single word at a time. In some way, this approach enables you to concentrate the brain on the written ideas instead of the words themselves. This is an ideal method for someone looking to improve their understanding of reading and their reading speed. You will greatly minimize the magnitude of the task your brain has to do when reading by soaking up whole ideas in a single moment. Rather than having to join words together to make a thought, your brain can understand the thinking at once by adding many words at once. This strategy will require some getting acquainted with, and it may not be for everybody.

Skimming

The last strategy of speed reading worthy of remembering is skimming. Mastering how to skim will allow you to discern the substance of a specific piece of writing without needing to take your time and effort to read the entire piece. This is a lot like comparison shopping for results, in a fashion. You skim through the products offered when you do comparison shopping, searching for items that are important to you. This is exactly the purpose of skimming written texts. You literally skim through a text, looking for the important material. You will have the capacity to identify valuable details in any document in a very little amount of time when you master how to skim. For everyone that wants to carry out research in some capacity, this is extremely useful. Many skimming strategies involve browsing the table of contents, book titles, blurbs and captions of images, and other related texts that are highlighted.

How to Assess and Monitor Progress in Speed Reading

Typically, the strategies of measuring speed and comprehension are quite simple, needing so little in respect of instruments or time. Nevertheless, what is crucial is that you spend some time periodically document your progress. Not only can these outcomes reflect the improvement you are having, but they will equally demonstrate any places that you are failing.

You will have the ability to reorganize your speed reading practice through being able to identify points where improvement is smallest, preferring approaches that explicitly target any places where you have difficulty.

The first step you have to take is to pick what you like to store these details in. Most individuals prefer a standard journal in which their reading speed and comprehension grades are registered. Journals are both affordable and easy to apply while still being rather compact in order for you to keep a record of your improvement in speed reading even when on the go. There are, nevertheless, individuals who favor a more modern form of performance tracking. Instead of physical journals, they prefer to use digital alternatives, such as excel spreadsheets or basic word packages.

Chapter 3:
Memory Improvement

Developing Better Brains

The Secret to The Creation of Better Brains

All the things we learn goes to the brain via our sense organs. However, the brain has designed barriers to the input of sensory data. It's an incredible organ. However, the billions of pieces of info bombarding it each second can't be processed. It is fitted with filters to shield itself from information congestion and concentrate on the information most important for survival in order to cope with the bombardment.

How the brain of an individual reacts to external sensory input dictates what information his attention receives. To access a person's thinking brain, just specified information goes via his lower brain filter (known as the reticular activating system, or RAS). When determining which sensory data to enable into the thinking brain, the RAS is especially sensitive to the excitement, shock, colour, and unforeseen/curious events.

When data makes it through the first filter, there is another filter in a section of the brain named the amygdala. The amygdala is a component of the connection of the limbic system of emotion processing. At the moment an individual receives the data, how well they store the sensory data that makes it past the amygdala filter is heavily affected by their emotional state. Whenever stress is high, the amygdala deflects the data to the automated reflex system, where non-thinking responses, such as fight/flight, are predominant. The knowledge is transferred on to the brain's cognitive, memory-making, and thinking channels whenever the amygdala is in a healthy state and feelings are optimistic.

There is something that allows sensory input to make it past these two filters, a biochemical neurotransmitter named dopamine. Dopamine is released if learning is connected with enjoyment. This surge boosts concentration, allowing the brain to remain active.

Knowing the way information reaches the brain to become knowledge and long-term memory as a mother is a useful weapon for enhancing an individual's brainpower. Applying brain-friendly techniques enriches you in adapting to the environment's most valuable sensory feedback and transforming that information into stored knowledge.

RAD Learning

There are two important brain mechanisms and three major brain structures that are crucial to developing powerful brains.

Patterning and neuroplasticity are the mechanisms. The three systems are what I call RAD, which is an abbreviation for:

- R: Reticular Activating System (RAS)
- A: Affective filter in the amygdala
- D: Dopamine

The Reticular Activating System (RAS)-Sensory Switchboard of the Brain

The RAS is the switching mechanism for attention control situated on the brain's lower end (brain stem). It gets feedback from the nerves converging into the spinal cord from nerve cells in the hands, legs, chest, neck, face, and vital organs. The RAS controls the remainder of the brain's level of euphoria and awareness. The RAS systematically signals brains to modifications that affect their survival, sounds, sights, and smells that could suggest risk or signal opportunities for food, mates, or shelter.

The RAS has developed in people to be receptive to more than simply the fundamental requirements for natural survival, though it is still a most sensitive filter to shifts in our climate. The RAS is crucial to "turning on" the degree of response and awareness of our brain.

The RAS's reaction to the sensory input it gets defines frequency, content, and kind of data accessible to the "higher" brain. Though the RAS is bombarded each waking second by billions of pieces of sensory information, this filter restricts access to around two thousand pieces each second.

In good learning, individuals are encouraged to pay attention to significant details by gaining their RAS's attention. Paying attention to lectures and conducting exercises and worksheets are not new or engaging activities. Therefore they do not provide enough mental stimuli to power data via the brain filters of the RAS.

The Amygdala, Where Heart Meets Mind

The sensory data that an individual acquires, the kinds of stuff he sees, hears, sounds, smells, or touches, activates their brain's absorption centers outside the RAS.

Sensory cortical regions in every lobe of the brain are the regions most involved anytime new data first reaches the brain. Any of these areas is designed to assess data from a single sense only (hearing, touch, taste, vision, and smell). This input is defined and graded by comparing it with already preserved similar information. For instance, the glimpse of citrus interacts with the visual cortex in the occipital lobes. In the parietal lobes, the texture of the citrus is identified by the somatosensory (touch) cores.

This sensory information then moves via the brain's psychological center, the limbic network, particularly the amygdala and hippocampus, wherein psychological meaning is correlated with data (sweet taste is yummy in citrus but yucky in unsweetened citrus juice). These psychological filters determine its enjoyment quality upon obtaining sensory information. The decision shows whether more entry to the higher brain is granted to the data and, if so, where the information would go.

These brain filter areas enter into awareness mode and redirect the sensory information away from the conscious brain and right into the automated centers (fight/flight) whenever the brain senses danger or an individual feels overwhelmed. Since there are generally no tigers in our homes, individuals don't actually require the same danger-filter answer as their prehistoric ancestors did. Yet, these filters still function in human brains and may be triggered in certain situations by the kind of stresses an individual encounters. These filters can be caused by bullying, concentration problems, misunderstanding, or boredom, preventing sensory information absorption relevant to learning. Since the sensations are seen as unpleasant interactions, the fight/flight reaction is involved, and learning gets difficult.

Dopamine, Working to Prime Your Brain

Dopamine is among the most significant neurotransmitters in the human brain. (Serotonin, tryptophan, acetylcholine, and norepinephrine are several of the many neurotransmitters in the human brain.) Such neurotransmitters are brain biochemicals that bring data across the gaps (synapses) that develop anytime one end of the neuron interacts with another. The human brain produces thirty thousand synapses each second per square centimeter of the cortical surface over the last trimester of embryonic development.

Anytime an event is enjoyable, the brain produces dopamine. As a delight-seeking organ, the brain often produces dopamine. This has many benefits in anticipation of satisfying, enjoyable events.

Dopamine production enhances attentive concentration and memory growth. During pleasant learning experiences, when dopamine is produced, it effectively enhances an individual's capacity to manage attention and preserve long-term memories.

Physical activity, individual interest links, social interactions, songs, excitement, the feeling of accomplishment, inherent gratification, preference, game, and amusement include learning experiences that may trigger dopamine production and generate satisfying experiences in the brain. To improve attention and concentration, the dopamine produced at the time of these exercises is then accessible.

How The Brain Develops Memory

An individual learns as their brain transforms sensory feedback into memory. The creation of new memories helps their brain to learn and anticipate the result of their actions through experience. Memory is a survival necessity for animals who have to learn, preserve, and remember the manner to react to physical requirements and shifts in their environment.

They restore preserved memories to remember and foresee. Where did they go to get their food? Where was the secure place that offered shelter? What areas were unsafe due to various predators

Every time an individual recalls something, he equally reactivates a neural circuit already generated by his brain. The neural network for that sequence or class of knowledge becomes broader as he incorporates new memories linked to knowledge previously in the brain bank as more links develop among nerve cells. In essence, the more knowledge accumulated in the circuits of the brain, the better we react to our situations more effectively. The more we learn, the more data preserved in our neural circuits, the more probable it is for our brains to react to new knowledge, so learning facilitates learning.

Learning Promotes Learning

The nerves that fit together are wired together. There is a high potential for more learning as more bonds develop between nerves. Some number of nerves are stimulated every time you engage in some endeavor. The same nerves react again if the activity is replicated, such as practicing music or evaluating a list. The more time an event (practice) is replicated or the data (review) is remembered, the more synapses grow to attach new memories to existing ones (plasticity), the greater the nerve attachments become, and the more effective the brain gets to restore or replicate the memory.

The learning exercises in this book will create better brains by enhancing the ability of an individual to choose the sensory feedback to concentrate on (RAS), driving the relevant knowledge via the brain filters (RAS and amygdala), and linking learning with positive experiences (dopamine release). An individual will create and preserve lasting cognitive memories via games that establish efficient patterning. With fun, learning force, compatible review activities, an individual brain's neuroplasticity can create more powerful neural networks from which to preserve and restore long-term memories. Each process of brain-empowering makes way for the next achievement because learning encourages learning.

Constructing lifelong learning is a wonderful cycle.

Sustaining a Healthy Brain

When we study six books a year, try crossword puzzles on the tunnel, and try some arithmetic without applying the calculator, we normally think that we are doing our best to stay mentally healthy. However, things have changed these days.

Mental exercises such as those listed above are still outstanding exercises and are being adopted by hundreds, though new research shows that we can try some other mental and physical workouts to sustain our gray matter in a perfect form.

Do you realize those innocent times of our adolescents when we had a vivid imagination and might quickly conjure up circumstances and attempt to play? Those times we tell our mates, "Do you like to play with me today," we are obviously inviting them to take part in whatever imagination is cooking in our brains ("You're the doctor, I'm the nurse, and since she has a stomach upset, we need to heal little Sue"). It was a fantastic period in life, and our enthusiasm and our feeling of exploration loaded us with difficulties.

Our whole early life was just like an explosion of lightning and an entertaining sequence of upward learning that developed our imaginations and strengthened our brains.

Mental Exercise

One important way to sustain brain health is by trying certain mental exercises, as we said previously. Suppose you use crosswords in your mind or measure figures, that's wonderful. Keep it up. I would also like to say that you should do the following activities, whether at school, in the workplace, in the cafe, in the car park, etc.

- **At School**

If a signpost explaining the meals for the day is in your lunchroom, make an attempt to go through it in detail and attempt to memorize the meals on the list. We appear to look at notice boards inattentively and do not properly comprehend anything as the detail is either insignificant or meaningless. Make reading the menu a regular habit and attempt to imagine ways to recollect whatever you have read.

- **In The Workplace**

When you're into languages, this ought to be a pleasing exercise. It's easier to have two brains than just one. You remember the saying! Many bilingual individuals have an advantage over their peers and colleagues who are unilingual. When they discover the corresponding word in a different language, they strain their minds and force them to work harder. Spanish is probably the second most commonly spoken language in the US, whereas

French is the most common language in Canada. Throughout the day, think of the Spanish or French version when you encounter people and see things in your company.

- **In The Restaurant**

You should take a close look at your waitress (or waiter) and take in his appearance, any unique moles, arm or eye movement, or if he has a ring. This is like doing a little investigative work, but it might not be a pleasant practice to do if you dine with your partner. Looking around the eatery and making an assumption as to how many clients there are in the building would be another great exercise. An option might be to find odd items in the restaurant and imagine that you have a magnetic memory, and memorize their location. You hone your awareness of hearing and sight in this way. It enables you to identify your position with respect to all the people and items that occupy the same environment by making a deliberate attempt to identify what is around you.

- **In The Car Park**

Several times, you might have worried about forgetting the place you left the car or thinking like your car was stolen. This often occurs in a big shopping complex in which the car parks are situated in the building's various quadrants. Try a mental record of all probable "aid finders" when parking your car: you are in column #, opposite a building (or road or a massive banner), the make and the paintings of the car on your left and right side, etc. In this manner, you will identify exactly where to head and what to look out for whenever you're finished with your buying and ready to take your leave. Rather than searching specifically for your car, you will locate the road signs, buildings, and the other cars that will enable you to identify your car's position. By trying this procedure on a daily basis, we will doubt that you will ever worry about the same thing!

A blogger on a website who posted a few mental workouts said that "any workout regimen that allows you to reflect is of benefit." You will be shocked to find out how easily the brain will react, and you will see an important change in your capacity to think easily, objectively, and dynamically in a really short period of time.

This author proposed this exercise as well. Focus on the license number of the car in front of you when driving. Note the license number on the plate and decrease it to one digit by adding all the numbers together. Add them when the outcome you get has more than a single digit. Repeat the addition until a single digit is reached.

Methodologies for Memory Improvement

Robert Allen has written a helpful memory improvement guide that definitely doesn't read like a technical guide close to the ones you get whenever you buy computer hardware or device.

He points out some strategies and real practices of art and creativity (and plenty of colour) about the manner to conserve power for your brain. This part will describe the general strategies that produce great benefits for us in the short and long run. You need not apply all of them. To improve your memory, pick a few or a minimum of one exercise to regularly try to improve your memory. One workout is better than none at all. As Robert Allen said, "When you begin today and learn, learn, learn, your memory will gradually be as effective as flypaper (although whatever gets stuck to it will, with a chance, be more valuable)."

It's a shame that our brains don't behave the same as machines. A brain-like machine would be a blessing to our everyday lives, wouldn't it? The human brain is much more sophisticated but not as stunning as a performer as a Pentium IV; but however it may not have the ability to spill out bits of data in seconds, the human brain has been at the heart of the evolution of mankind and culture. Memory is, therefore a very useful commodity and instrument. It's not mechanical; it's the material from which we're created.

We will quickly review two facets of memory before explaining concrete memory enhancement strategies: learning and concentration. Every individual has his unique manner of learning and concentrating. For memory development, such two ideas are major requirements. It involves the gathering of knowledge and real abilities, while concentration is the capacity of the brain to focus effectively on anything with the tiniest amount of interruption.

- **Learning**

Robert Allen says people learn in different ways: while looking, when listening and when doing. There are people who depend primarily on vision, some others on their ability to hear, and yet others who learn by actually doing. To determine one's most prevalent learning approach, such measures exist. We will deal with each of these realistic assessments briefly:

After spending some time watching a movie, for example, what aspect do you recollect the most-the conversation, the action scenes, or the stuff you did, such as going to the theater, purchasing a movie ticket, and ice cream? If "conversation" is your response, that renders you to be a listener. You will be a looker when you replied to "action scenes," and when you responded to the "things you did," that renders you to be a doer.

A further illustration: how will you navigate your way around when you just moved to a new region: (a) ask the residents for guidance, (b) acquire a navigation map, or (c) move around the city to acquaint yourself with the region's structure? If you replied (a), you're going to be a listener, you're a looker when you selected (b), and you will be a doer if you picked (c).

Of course, to decide the manner in which an individual learns and what kind of learner they are, we require more experimental tests: a listener, a looker, or a doer. Five or thirty queries would not lead to an accurate evaluation, but Allen's illustrations at least provide an estimate of his principle of learning; and learning is an important component of memory, as we discussed earlier.

A person that enjoys sounds, particularly words, and sees strong meanings in them is a learner that listens. Listeners prefer to recall better, instead of via any other sensory experience, what they have processed by their ability to hear. On the contrary, Lookers respond better to external stimulation to easily interpret and remember everything they observe. People that enjoy rolling up their sleeves and digging into the mud are the doers. They emphasize practical knowledge; for them, there is more sense in doing things practically.

Allen claims that learning things solely in one fashion is uncommon for anybody. He notes that integrating all the learning styles and adapting everyone to a specific circumstance will be the best method of attack.

- **Concentration**

You may have the greatest memory-enhancing trainer, but it will be hard to have much of a successful memory when you cannot concentrate. It is hard to concentrate; consider how much electronics have taken over our existence. Allen claims there is only one strategy in the memory-training classes he took during his career that could help other people improve their concentration abilities. He states that this one is borrowed from a Far Eastern society and is a couple of decades tradition, but still precious. This sounds simple enough, but your initial attempts to do it can seem ineffective:

Light some candles and put them on a table where you are able to see them clearly; Look at the candles and notice each detail in two minutes: color, wax, size, flame, etc.; Cover your eyes and maintain the candle picture in the center of your mind, keep this picture for as long as you can;

Resist to be distracted by your first effort or your second. Continue attempting until you can hold the picture of the candle for as long as you are able to. Now that we have described the two basic components for developing your memory, let's "focus" on the ways to develop our memory:

What do you believe is the most basic concept for enhancing your memory? Allen explicitly states it. Pay attention to yourself!

The body and mind are together an entity. Don't assume that you should go about trying things you like to do and ignore your real body in your happy way. Allen states that the following rules are stuff you encounter frequently. Ancient advice but great advice, so pay attention to them:

- **Adequate Sleep**

An obstacle to focus and learning is not getting adequate sleep. Were you as effective at the workplace or in school on such days when you had inadequate rest and sleep? Have you recalled and retained more, or have you felt a sluggish brain?

- **Balanced Diet**

The specialists have emphasized, again and again, that a healthy and nutritious meal is a remedy for strained and burned-out lives. For our brain to work at an optimum level, decent nutrition is important. How do we anticipate our brain to be at its best efficiency without the energy our body requires? Your tray should be packed with fresh food and vegetables. Individuals that eat breakfast have increased memory abilities, according to studies, than those individuals who miss this essential food of the day.

- **Fresh Air**

Try to respire properly, be mindful of the air quality in your homes and workplaces, and profit from the fresh air. This implies that we ought to have a window open as wide as possible when working, keeping a decent temperature in the room. Our focus and mental functioning skills are compromised by stale air, which is prevented from circulating properly.

- **Physical Exercise**

Not very many individuals enjoy aerobic exercise or heavy-lifting. Consider going for long walks or swimming laps, if you're one of them. The idea is to work-out a minimum of 30 minutes per session some days of the week.

- **Alcohol and Tobacco**

Oh, hell NO! Our perception, focus, and memory can be affected by the popular "hang-over" we experience right after a night of drinking and "partying." Eradicate drinking and smoking from your schedule, particularly when you do it excessively so that your memory works. An infrequent slip-up can create a simple memory blip, but in numerous horrible ways, extended violence may screw up your mind. Memory failure is definitely going to be one of them.

Analytical Thinking

An author describes it this way: critical thinking comes in whenever we reason through attention and deliberation. It is neither basic logic nor is it instinct. The very same author argues that anytime we examine, prepare and describe, we think critically. The scientific approach is all centered on orderly, critical thinking. We analyze critically anytime we assess, quantify and record information. We employ critical logic whenever we pay our bills.'

By comparison, reflective thought is when we reflect on our knowledge objectively and go through the depths of our rational gut feelings. Therefore, we analyze our ideas and bring them to the level of critical thinking as we indulge in reflective thinking. Therefore, critical thought is triggered and established by constant usage.

These comments do not really explain the difference, but it's a great start. We searched for another critical thought concept, something which undergraduates will go through this period, because professors typically ask them to basically evaluate everything they have studied.

Analytical thinking allows students to define exactly what the main argument is in a document from the viewpoint of a reader, to reflect on the reasoning and validity of the claims, to comment on the way the claim is portrayed, and then to challenge the reliability of the proof supporting the claim(s)

Chapter 4: NLP Tips & Techniques For Faster Learning

Understanding the Fundamentals

The first secret to comprehending NLP can be seen in the buzzwords of its name. The fundamental theory of NLP is that both verbal and non-verbal (linguistic) will influence the attitude and habits you use to accomplish your goals by connecting the neurological process in your system (neuro) to the language you employ (programming).

Neurology

Neurology implies the human nervous system functioning. Prior to focusing on that, we have to especially look at the elements of the nervous system, primarily the central nervous system, that is accountable for the instinctive habits taken in swift, unpredictable circumstances that do not need pre-processing, and then after the peripheral nervous system, that is accountable for the simple acts of thought, storing and categorizing knowledge and preparing and executing actions.

An individual's nervous system is the device that the system uses to feel the environment around it and then analyze it within the brain. The five main senses are used by the system:

auditory, stimuli, kinesthetic, olfactory, and optical. The internal mind will process the external world by the use of the ears, tongue, skin and motion, nose, and eyes.

Now we can have a look at the manner in which the CNS works. The CNS is the core of the whole of the ideas, decisions, and perceptions of a human being. Anytime in a circumstance, our central nervous system assesses the circumstance in which it discovers itself and performs those acts on the basis of one of the below ideas, causing our system to respond in a specific manner:

- Based on past occurrences: It is possible to call upon encounters that have been stored in our memory to direct the brain in making certain decisions in related circumstances.
- Based on the surrounding context: The human mind presents a profoundly embedded response in the upbringing we have been through in situations in which there is no previous knowledge of an incident and the setting in which the human being has been exposed.

As is obvious, anything from previous knowledge to the world is processed in the human mind and influences our way of thought. Because of this, two people can discover themselves using radically distinct approaches to how to manage this circumstance in related situations. This variation exists largely because of the disparity in perception.

This makes it necessary to have the ability to efficiently and effectively categorize and recover these details. This is where NLP helps.

Language

The next element in NLP is linguistics. Linguistics is the knowledge of the language in rudimentary terms. Here, it relates to the mechanism used to communicate our opinions and express our ideas in action. Language is perhaps the most critical aspect of reaching an efficient and practical target, although it might sound overestimated.

The creation of the language used by an individual is dependent on the product of the details processed by the senses. For data from the sense of hearing, context and perception are provided as sound, gustatory as taste, sense of skin as a feeling, sense of nose as smell, and visual as pictures. Via language, such interpretations are then articulated, verbal and nonverbal.

One of the big disadvantages facing individuals recently is that of poor communication. They cannot accurately articulate their thoughts, and even though they try, they ultimately end up talking before reflecting. This also contributes to a mixed response from the communication partner and, therefore, inhibits the sender's brain's productivity. While this applies to outside communication, inner communication should also be provided the same value, like in the context of the human brain, there is a constant and persistent monologue, whether during judgment or while interpreting a circumstance. Inner communication has to be transparent, detailed, and reliable for this purpose.

Programming

They have to be organized together until the brain and the linguistics have been programmed to deliver the maximum results required to train the mind to function in the best feasible manner, that is achieved by programming, and to maintain control over our brain & language.

To optimize the brain's productivity, the first action is to assemble our opinions, perceptions, and ideas. "As the adage goes, "A congested mind is the workspace of the devil"! A congestion in the system's storage space may at awkward times contribute to unnecessary, unnecessary emotional responses, thus hindering an individual's effectiveness, whether in professional or private fields.

It is here that programming supports a healthy feeling, preventing them from intervening in a specific circumstance in which it is not necessary. It often occurs that the human mind may also often get overwhelmed about the way to generate the precise information needed in a circumstance because of an accumulation of knowledge. In such a scenario, programming helps to compartmentalize and categorize stored details so that it is possible to maximize the recovery of information.

The programming is the overall outcome of the manner your emotions, feelings, and behaviors are structured from the perception of your senses and made evident by your language. It will be reflected in your actions, which creates modifications in the external world.

For instance, a worker is on his table, which is loaded with documentation that has to be organized and recorded the following day. Sensations are bombarding his senses, watching his manager speak to him on how important he wants the tasks completed and also watching the clock tick away second by second. He then draws a deep breath and informs his colleague that he will never be able to complete the job on the stipulated time. He speaks to himself that his mission is a hopeless case after all of his colleagues leave, and he may equally give up, head home, and abandon the job undone. He fails to finish his assignment after his work shift and heads home.

The premise underlying NLP is that assuming he had handled his circumstance in a different frame of mind and in a better language, the worker may have been able to complete his mission. His frame of mind ought to have been one of success and accomplishment, rather than feeling lost. He ought to have used language which is hopeful of performance rather than using terms that imply failure. In NLP, it is not the clock nor the volume of work that led to the loss, however the worker himself or, more precisely, his actions due to his frame of mind and mode of language.

Consequently, progress can be accomplished not by initially altering the external world but by altering the world inside you. You can script yourself with an acceptable or preferred attitude by regaining control of the way you perceive the information given by your sensory system and the manner you put such meanings into words. Due to the alterations in your internal world, if you have changed your actions, the outside world surrounding you will alter as a result of it.

Strategies Applied in Neuro-Linguistics Programming

Presumptions

NLP employs assumptions that act as the basis for its strategies. These assumptions describe the perception of the physiological, lingual, and behavioral world by NLP, both your personal and the separate environment of other individuals.

Such assumptions give further insight into the central concepts of NLP as well. Notice that these are only a few of the several

NLP presumptions; similar presumptions will exist for any particular use of NLP in a specific area, for instance, in an organizational or therapeutic environment. A few of the more common assumptions that are relevant to a broad range of fields are those mentioned below. A few of these presumptions are as follows:

- The map is never the region. NLP thinks that we will never truly understand or grasp reality as human beings. Our knowledge of the environment around us is defined, and only our interpretation of truth can perceive it. We can solely depend on our sensory as humans to perceive reality. This implies that in NLP, our conduct is dictated by this conceptual map, not the real physical territory itself. Thus, it is not truth itself that inhibits or enables us to achieve our goals or achieve achievement, rather our personal expectations.
- All tool for success is inside you. This is an essential expansion of the previous premise. This suggests that you already hold the key to achieve success because it is not the outside reality, rather your inner view of reality that can impede or promote success. There is a tremendous amount of unrealized potential inside each of us that can generate the success that everyone needs. Just a few individuals have successfully tapped into their capacity for success, including those successful

individuals that the founders have researched. You can be directed into accessing your reservoir via NLP.

- The Required Variety Principle. It states that the individual with the greatest versatility in his or her actions will have the greatest influence over the world. This implies that you need to have power over your circumstance to accomplish your target. The more you possess choices, the more power you will exercise. In NLP, you are advised to provide a range of solutions to a specific issue or a series of steps in line with a target objective. This is because the environment around us varies, and if you have more than a single choice, solution, or move, you should adapt and be versatile as the circumstances warrant. This manner, if one strategy you use does not yield your desired outcome, go for another.
- No failure occurs, just feedback. There is a permanent state of self-confidence in the ever-evolving sub-systems and systems in that we all belong. Any adjustments implemented in the framework would produce waves of change aimed at integrating the adjustment and restoring equilibrium once again. This implies that if you fail to fix your problem, it is not necessarily a failure but instead a suggestion from the system that your approach is unacceptable.

Anchoring

Anchoring or self-anchoring entails forming a link between a feeling and a stimulation. Anchors imply stimuli that activate specific feelings and stimuli. The scent of freshly baked cake, for instance, restores infancy memories. A traumatic experience is caused by the scent of fire. A contact may bring soothing images to mind. Anger elicits a red traffic signal. Alertness is stimulated by a flashing red light. Such anchors are usually involuntary. Without the person becoming conscious of the stimulus, the awareness of such unique sensations arouses feelings, experiences, and emotions.

A beneficial emotional condition in NLP is connected to physical stimulation. The Pavlovian theory of conditioning is a perfect example. When it senses food, a dog froths. The dog is anchored to another stimulation that produces the same response (frothing). Any time food is served, a bell sounds. With time, the dog anchored the awareness of food to a bell's echo. Any time it sees the bell ringing, the dog begins to froth at the mouth. Therefore, the froth is anchored to the ringing bell.

In humans, similar conditioning could be carried out. A unique sensation is anchored to physical stimulation. The power of anchors to evoke feelings and emotions is harnessed by NLP. It strives at anchoring triggers into emotions and feelings that are more constructive and productive. To excite pleasure, trust and enhanced capacity, stimuli could be conditioned. If faced with bad emotions and circumstances, this strategy helps an individual to elicit optimistic and pleasant emotions and thoughts. It's just like inducing hopeful feelings in demand.

Things You Have to Note While Using NLP

Although there are no adverse impacts on the NLP, certain adverse impacts are likely to occur over the course of the procedure. Nevertheless, this is not the situation. When experimenting with NLP, certain precautionary steps have to be taken that hinder the strategy from going wrong, leading to catastrophic final results.

Since the basis of the strategy is based on the principle of contrast, it is vital not to go excessive by overstating other individuals or underestimating one's personal skill, as this results in a total deviation from the program's objective. Keeping yourself on a high plinth may equally have belittling consequences, as a criticism of oneself is a significant feedback evaluation measure for any personal development scheme.

NLP centers mainly on the management of thoughts and feelings by control measures. NLP enables you to maintain concentration and organisation by managing feelings and behavior. Nevertheless, this ought to be done within boundaries, as a total absence of emotions can render an individual cold and cruel and ruin one's interactions and relationships with others. Overusing or showing them in unacceptable conditions hampers development and must therefore be prevented. Be your brain's master, don't allow it to boss you.

Emphasis is crucial to bringing meaningful results out of the plan, so prior to starting, it is important to have a specific objective in mind. As stated before, objectives can be changed, but too frequent changes can result in a confused and troubled mind. Consider concentrating on achieving the objective in its initial form once a target has been identified, instead of changing it based on your preferences each time. The NLP is a scientific framework that works on factual analysis and, as a result, ought to be approached as one.

At the beginning of the program, do NOT anticipate results. The NLP system performs with respect to one's capacity, and the amount of time taken to show outcomes differs from individual to individual, as every person is made differently.

Therefore, increasing your standards could result in frustrations and a declining excitement that could appear fatal for mind control. It is important to avoid loophole methods and disturbances at all costs, as this would only further delay the system's development.

Chapter 5:
Boosting Your IQ

The Meaning of IQ

Intelligence quotient (IQ) is a function of specialists' mental qualities that make up human intelligence: especially rationality, logic, fast-thinking, and information. A contrast of intelligence between individuals is made possible by measuring these abilities. Only straightforward? It's definitely not.

- **Is IQ the Same as Intelligence?**

IQ can appear to be a defined object since it can be evaluated and ascribed a value. But what was really tested, and what does the outcome demonstrate about our general capacity to reflect and reason?

Also, scientists are yet to completely agree about what IQ entails and the way it can be measured precisely. It is not always simple to identify the distinctions between innate abilities and acquired skills. Ways to assess subtleness in intellectual capacity are continually being developed, and assessments are designed to eradicate as many cultural differences and perception uncertainty as possible. However, challenges exist in aspects like basic knowledge and grammar. Due to the effects of restricting so much variability within a human brain to a single amount, the validity of IQ has also been fiercely argued.

- **IQ as a Metric of Accomplishment**

Certain generalizations on the connection between IQ and accomplishment are given by figures and, more adversely, IQ and societal issues. Great IQ is also reflected in education, university, and job success, with individuals whose IQ scores are in the top 5 percent continuing to receive the largest earning. On the other hand, individuals whose IQs are below 5% are significantly more likely to develop social issues, violate the rules, and go to jail: they find it more of a challenge in life, whereas more mean IQ scorers excel optimizing their ability. This doesn't nullify IQ checks, nevertheless. Although they may not provide a full picture of intelligence, the abilities they assess are essential for far more than formal learning and career growth.

But an IQ score is centered on a specific set of skills, whereas performance and fulfillment come from a broad range of internal and acquired skills that enable us to be flexible and successful at what we do. There are individuals with very great IQs who have struggled in life, whereas by optimizing their ability, more average IQ-scorers succeed. This doesn't nullify IQ checks, nevertheless. Although they may not provide a full picture of intelligence, the abilities they assess are essential, for far greater than formal learning and professional growth.

Testing of IQ

From numerous activities that have been specially designed for health or educational reasons to simplified models tailored to the office to those performed for pleasure, IQ tests are in different shapes. Both of them, nevertheless, require similar skills.

- **The Scale of Wechsler**

The Wechsler Intelligence is the most commonly accepted IQ measure (WAIS). "The American scientist David Wechsler designed the test. He defined intelligence in 1939 as "the people's global ability to act deliberately, think logically, and cope properly with his (or her) setting.

This is probably the measure applied by health professionals to determine a person's intellectual capacity, for instance, after a sudden stroke or brain problem. A kid's version, the Wechsler Intelligence Scale for Children (WISC), is applied in schools.

This form of a complete IQ test is built not solely to measure an individual's general intellectual ability but also to display strengths and weaknesses in particular aspects, such as a better-than-average logical thinking capacity or a higher facility with numbers than with words.

The WAIS tests 14 facets of capacity, split into four domains, or categories, to provide the most precise image possible of mental prowess:

- The speed of reasoning (capacity to absorb and process details swiftly and precisely)
- Cognitive enterprise (capacity to identify visual patterns and perceive information)
- Verbal interpretation (grammar, the capacity to structure and express details in words)
- Working memory (ability to remember and arrange letter and/or number series sequences).

The pace of processing and perceptual organization is seen to be essentially innate. On the other hand, verbal interpretation is strongly affected by educational resources, both formal and informal. Working memory, which requires arithmetical calculation and the way things are remembered, is something that we will look at later in-depth, as recent research has shown that this is key to improving IQ capacity.

Mastering to Think Straight

Previous experience has an effect on the way we treat new detail or address new questions. We will improve our odds of a new, precise approach by identifying habitual errors in our thought and taking action to rectify them, including unlearning our normal belief that certain cognitive problems are out of our control.

Handling Distortion

Habitual variations in the manner we think of ourselves may inadvertently weaken our brain capacity. This can serve as a self-fulfilling forecast if we have a low perception of our personal intellectual capacity, weakening our belief and as a result leading to a bad outcome in a specific mental challenge. We shape mental constructs called "schemas" through practice to direct us instinctively through a broad range of daily activities, from making household profiles to participating in a political debate over lunch with colleagues. But not all schemas are beneficial: in manners that contribute to underperformance, they may alter our expectations.

Knowing Bad Schemas

American scientist Jeffrey Young described 18 potential bad schemes, separated into five main categories relating to our interactions with ourselves and other individuals (a popular cause of distress).

Strategies Capable of Boosting Your IQ

Human intelligence is composed of two broad sections: fluid intelligence and crystallized intelligence. Conceptual thinking is connected with fluid intelligence, while crystallized intelligence is linked with the formation of intellectual abilities.

Such forms of intelligence could be affected by a number of hereditary and external factors. According to the National Library of Medicine, they include:

- IQ of parents
- The Genes
- Life at home
- Type of parenting
- Balanced Diet
- Education

Below are some things that you can try to boost your intelligence in different fields, from thinking and organising to problem-solving, etc.

Activities of The Memory

Not solely memory, but also thought and language abilities can be improved by memory exercises. Memory games have actually been applied in certain organizational study experiments to investigate how memory relates to knowledge of languages and artifacts. Reasoning and language are also adopted as tests of intelligence, suggesting that intelligence will keep improving memory tasks.

Activities that help in training the memory include:

- Puzzles
- Puzzles with Crosswords
- Board games or card matching
- Sudoku

Executive Control Activities

Executive control is the power to regulate high cognitive tasks. It is a portion of the Trusted Source executive feature that also involves executive management and compliance. Research shows that executive control, one component of human intelligence, is closely tied to fluid thinking.

Activities that have to do with executive control training are:

- Scrabble
- Pictionary
- Red light, green light
- Puzzle

Activities of Visuospatial Thinking

The cognitive process relating to physical depictions is involved in visuospatial thinking. Scientists discovered in a study that enhancing visuospatial thinking contributed to an improvement in IQ test performance. Memory and executive function exercises were partially employed in that research to help develop individuals' visuospatial thinking.

Activities involving visual and spatial guidance include:

- Mazes
- Activities of point-of-view
- Models in 3-D
- Prisms that are unfolded

Relational Abilities

The relational Frame Concept applies to the growth of human reasoning and language by relational comparisons. A study from 2011 has proved that it can substantially increase children's IQ performance by using the Relational Frame concept as a strategy.

Enhancements in IQ, verbal thinking, and numerical reasoning were also identified in a more latest research using this strategy.

Relational training events include:

- Articles on learning languages ("this is a..." and "that is a...")
- Comparative analysis of Objects (filled cup against empty cup)
- Comparative analysis of Quantity (penny versus dime)

The Musical Equipment

To profit from mastering a musical instrument, you need not have to be the next popular musician. One research showed that there is greater working memory for musicians than for non-musicians.

Considering the significant role memory performs in intelligence, eventually picking up that musical instrument you've often liked to learn can boost your IQ.

New Languages

Will you be shocked to understand that more than half of the world's largest Trusted Source mass is bilingual? This should appear with no marvel that the human brain benefits from learning numerous languages, and the faster, the better.

The connection between advanced language learning and IQ was explored in a new study by Trusted Source. The findings showed that language training was most helpful for intellectual results later in adulthood through speech and communication from 18 to 24 months.

Reading Regularly

In human mental growth, there is no doubt how useful books can be. In fact, if books form an aspect of parental bonding practices, the advantages of growth are even more noticeable.

In a new Trusted Source report, scientists found that infants had higher language and mental development abilities if parents read aloud to their infants.

Continued Education

Education, in any manner, is vital to the growth of human intelligence. More than 600,000 individuals were examined in a study of Trusted Source on IQ and education to assess education's impact on IQ performance. The scientists discovered that individuals recorded a boost of two to six IQ areas for each extra year of formal education.

Role of Meditation

It is quite simple to get overwhelmed with knowledge and ideas, all sorts of noise, events, and errands in this modern era where everyone appears to be in a hurry or on their devices. The outcome? On so many days, we are exhausted, our minds function in overdrive, and our wellbeing struggles.

There are a lot of methods of combating stress, and meditation is surely one of them. Meditation is performed to prepare the brain, taking us back to the current time and offering us an incentive not just to ourselves but also to other individuals to be more relaxed and kinder.

- **Mindfulness Meditation**

In the last couple of years, a meditation on mindfulness has increasingly gained popularity. It focuses on helping you to alleviate tension and increase tranquility and peace. The specialist gives full concentration to the current period without judgement in this form of meditation.

A popular misunderstanding is that meditation implies clearing the brain, but it simply enables us to concentrate on physical emotions, perceptions, and opinions to understand them more clearly.

- **Meditate to Improve Your IQ**

In relieving anxiety, reducing blood pressure, and enhancing the mind, meditation is helpful. Nevertheless, are you aware that meditating frequently can improve your memory and IQ as well?

- **Boost Your Memory**

An Awareness and Intelligence research showed that individuals who meditated for over three days for 20 minutes exhibited decreased stress levels and substantial changes in remembrance and cognition. Individuals that meditated equally scored as many as ten times higher on a working memory activity.

Experts at UC Santa Barbara discovered in another research that two weeks or more of meditation on cognition could substantially improve working memory capability, understanding of learning, and capacity to concentrate. You may direct this emphasis to practice towards becoming a professional financial analyst with CFI's Financial Modeling and Valuation Analyst (FMVATM) Certification program.

- **Increase Your IQ**

A neurofeedback study on this subject was performed by Siegfried Othmer, past head of the neurofeedback unit of the Association for Applied Psychophysiology and Biofeedback. The findings revealed that people that meditated demonstrated a mean 23 percent increase in IQ.

One of the factors is that cognitive function is slowed down by strong meditation. The brain enhances its capacity to reconfigure itself with weaker brainwaves. It strengthens itself anytime you offer your brain some relaxation.

The stress hormone referred to as cortisol is minimized essentially by regulating your breath. It emphasizes negative problems as the mind saunters, which can contribute to stress. With meditation, the mind is less busy and thus decreases levels of stress.

Consider Meditation

Wish to consider meditation? There are plenty of methods, to begin with. Try the Insight Timer app that will lead you through the system if you're going down the digital road. It equally makes it easier for you to monitor your development. You can as well practice personally. Begin by sitting and concentrating on your breath with your eyes shut. You may also enjoy some relaxing songs.

Chapter 6:
Boosting Your Ability To Learn

Your Current Study Pattern

Consider this 3-Minute study habit Test

- Are you really living up to the full capacity you have?
- Are you forcing out the ultimate greatest accomplishment that will offer you your inherent intelligence? In other words, are you being supported or hindered by your current learning habits?
- From the very first moment you open a book, is your brain's power harnessed or blocked every step of the way?

This three-minute item-list will show you right away. It's a fast, analytical measure, not of your intellect or skill, but of the outcomes that your current learning habits may offer you. Logically observe your learning patterns for a night. Then respond with a yes or a no to the below questions. Any weak point in your learning habit will become crystal clear to you in three short minutes. You're going to identify the pavement in your direction, and you're going to take the first move in eliminating them.

Find them below. Respond to them coldly and honestly.

Do you:

- Find it difficult to focus your eye on whatever you're reading?
- Are you having trouble choosing the key ideas of the book you're reading at each point in time?
- Forget whatever you read the evening right before the following day?
- Have difficulty locating books, pen, notebook, articles you.... like to work with?
- Do you need hours to get yourself started on the document you like to learn?
- Devote unfruitful time in corporate mathematics struggling to offer a solution to standard problems?
- Repeat the same errors over and over?
- Find difficulty putting your ideas on paper?
- Copy the reports, emails, and notes of others instead of creating your own?
- Forget new words in your vocabulary just as soon as you master them?
- Put up letters which are a disaster of scribbles and shredded pages that are unreadable?
- Never complete work on time?
- Badly cramming for advancement tests?
- Falling sick out of fear before those examinations?

What number of questions have you answered with a yes? This section would be worth much more to you than just the time you spend on it. If you have four affirmative yes responses, then you are wasting over 25 percent of your brain capacity via sloppy learning patterns. In other words, you receive a minimum of 25 percent lower marks than you ought to be provided by your inherent capacity. Such missed percentage points are restored by this book. And if you've had seven or above yes responses, you're in danger; you can see it in a glimpse, and you're in for an important life's most drastic and uncomplicated output changes.

Save the test. Review your replies to this post, in pen or pencil. Then, a week after, by the time you've completed this section and you've been running through the strategies mentioned, consider taking this test again at exactly that moment. Note down your latest responses, one week from now, against the old ones.

The disparity can drive you out of your breath. In reality, in that first week, you can observe yourself rising, watch your learning patterns shift, perceive yourself turning the corner to progress.

And if there are some yes responses left by the end of that time, then basically labelled those weak points. Once more, repeat the procedures over. And a month after, retake the test. Like water on a heated burner, you'll watch those yes responses disappear.

And you'll perceive the effects of these processes-in black and white:

- On the following ranking sheet
- In the eyes of your manager and colleagues
- On the kind of individual, you can now fascinate with your conversation
- On the kind of book, you can now read and repeat
- On the latest promotion, you've received
- Raise you've received
- Feeling of pure clear happiness you've picked up with your personal mind.

Our Plan of Approach for Better Learning Ability

A large number of individuals have been puzzled in the last couple of years. They became so obsessed with sociology, chemistry, linguistics, etc., that they overlooked how straightforward a great education is actually is.

A decent education, a cornerstone education, an education that may thrive or fail for the rest of your life consists of only three basic abilities:

- The capacity to read,
- The ability to articulate feelings in words, and
- The capacity to address mathematical issues.

The Three Basic foundation of Success

Reading, arithmetic, and writing. The ancient people recognized it. We equally have forgotten about it, and we need to return back to them. They are the building blocks. Every other thing else hinges on them, all the higher topics. If you cannot comprehend what you read, for instance, you can't study science.

You may not be able to write decent copies of ads if you can't articulate your own ideas. If elementary arithmetic does not fix simple issues, then you may not even be able to work on calculus or thermodynamics. For instance, all you work on in your professional life relies on your capacity to read, write, and calculate.

You'll be reading journals, reports, posts, and files for the most part of your career. You'll be writing emails, letters, suggestions, and performance reviews for the majority part of your life. You will sort out food bills, maintenance costs, loan repayments, and benefit and loss many times in your life. If you are not able to read like a pro, write like a genius, and calculate like a wizard, then you're going to waste everything else that you do with your brain.

Consequently, your basic task, the sole big key of a successful building into your career, is to ensure that in reading, writing and mathematics, you are a "blasting talent" And "I mean brilliant! We'll see your peers blown by your capacity to read a piece of text by the time we get done with that mind of yours, to churn out a detailed report, to cut through a computational dilemma to its very heart.

Reading, writing, and math. In every of these, you will make yourself an expert. And you will do it in ten short minutes per day, applying these three extremely strong tools: Fresh scientific methods, everyday practice, and the exciting feeling of achievement each time you learn something new! This is the manner they blend to get you off to a genius level, bang begin-today.

What You Read Has No Meaning Its Your Application

Your main challenge, therefore, is twofold. Firstly, you must understand the modern scientific methods of reading, writing, and mathematics. And secondly, each day, you need to put this knowledge into practical use, so you may ensure you've got them perfect. This is the simple punch that knocks hard topics into a cocked hat, shooting up the ability to learn faster.

This routine check-up approach is referred to as "feedback." in machine language. Engineers realize that it's not the information you input into a machine that matters; it's what the machine uses the information for, which is "feeds back" to you that matters. It is possible to lose, neglect, or misrepresent any of that data. You need to request it again to ensure accuracy.

The same thing goes for the mind. For each day of your existence, in all that you learn, the things you read actually means nothing. Words will literally go in and out of your head like liquid via a funnel. What stays with you is the sole thing that matters. That's the amount of what you comprehend. That's how many you recall. And how many you should put to practical use right away.

Let this reality sinks into your head. Mere reading is just the initial step in order to learn any topic. The bellow steps make up the full, efficient learning process:

- Reading,
- Comprehension,
- Remembering, and
- Reproducing the main ideas in your personal words.

This is the ultimate target you seek. Reproducing, the practical use, communicate in your personal words, be it in print or in discussion with your peers. (Or to solve new issues in the case of mathematics.) This is exactly what you are looking for, the final result. If your learning process falls short of this purpose, this precise expression of one feeling, then you get just half the value of your effort.

You've got to ensure you get it. Every single day, you need to use these amazingly effective modern learning strategies. This is how you're doing it.

The Role of Practice

Beginning today, and even each day you study this piece, try this: Spend a minimum of ten minutes every day to bring these modern learning strategies to practice. The day's period is irrelevant; but without disruptions and no feeling of urgency, you should be able to devote the time entirely to your practice, in full commitment to these new techniques.

Nothing in the universe counts over those few minutes per day but your imagination and the achievements it offers you! In ten minutes, this will be the moment you initially go through a journal article and frighten your mates the very same day by bouncing off each key idea it contains.

This is the first moment you unlock the gate to a fresh area of ideas that you have frequently dreamed of exploring philosophy, economics, science, software development, and discover that you may now brush over it-absorbing its details and concepts, like a sponge. Yeah, this is the moment in which you just realize that you may place words on paper that sing, that capture the mind of men, that alter their imaginations, that render them acting in the ways and manners you like them to behave!

You would practice not longer than fifteen minutes every day at the start. But then, as your capacity develops better and better as you develop more and more confidence in your personal ability to learn, you would like to dedicate more time every day to this exciting new idea for the expression of one's self and self-development. You will appreciate the true feeling of learning, maybe for the first time in your existence!

The Secret Ways to Word Power

Knowledge of words is the first prerequisite for being a great reader. As you study, you learn new vocabulary as you hear, as you acquire knowledge from all possible sources. Word-learning an important and probably the most significant component of your education. Since words are the instruments of thought.

Mental instruments that render thinking much simpler, much more accurate, much more successful in tackling the issues you face in your daily life. The more words you master, the more mental resources at your disposal to work with. The aim of this section is to present to you how these instruments can be learned.

The manner to make your interaction glow without knowing a new single word. Right away, let's attempt a short word game- that you could try in just a few minutes per day-anywhere-with the least vocabulary development preparation. A word game that will bring out of your "Secret Vocabulary Bank," dozens of Power-Packed words and set them to action for you immediately! Let us simply call this easy Change-the-Word-

Game activity a quest in your dialogue for alternative words, and watch the magic improvements you could achieve by the time you fit them in.

Take the glorious section from the Old Testament, for instance: "When they were in the field, Cain rose up against Abel and slew him." What might change if, in this statement, we modified the main words? Are we going to make this expression better? Are we going to add to the meaning or subtract from it? Tell yourself to understand it and try it.

Maybe you're going to substitute "rose up" with terms like collaborated against, despised blindly, assaulted treacherously. Maybe you're going to substitute "slew" for terms like killed, slaughtered, eviscerated, assassinated. Which is the most thrilling among these modern words? Which one most bears the idea? As you carry on, you learn to look for precisely the perfect word to express the color and sense of what you like to say. You feel at home with all sorts of words, small and big, plain and complex. To anything you say or compose, you blend in drama and scope. And almost instantly, you observe the difference in how individuals pause and react to you—and just you—when you start talking.

For like a week, attempt it. Assure yourself that " nice," "sweet," "exciting," "good," or any such familiar terms and phrases will never be used anymore. Look for new vocabulary full of passion, full of color, new ways of communicating your opinions, emotions, and desires. This single exercise solely will make a big impact on the influence that your words will have on those around you, and it's just the start.

Ways to Teach Yourself to Recognise Odd Words

You now have the ability to play the most fun, and lucrative game of all, mastering the way words are created. Realizing what the new words mean to look them up, not having to disrupt the flow of your reading. If you adopt this easy, two-step method, this might equally be an adventure in your learning: Firstly, you need to remember that each word is made up, bits and pieces, just like a model airplane is.

Words, although, are a lot more basic. They only compose of these three fundamental components:

- They usually have a base or stem that informs us the fundamental sense, like "go."
- Then we have the front element or prefix that attaches to the base word another meaning, such as "out" plus "go" is equivalent to "outgo."
- And finally, we have the ending part, or suffix, that offers us another definition. "For instance, "ing," that rounds our word out to provide us "out" plus "go" plus "ing" to add up to "outgoing.

Therefore, from three simple words, we may create a big word. So this provides us a fresh word that is less hard to recall. It requires far less space to compose and really provides us a new sense that we most probably wouldn't have had entirely with the three individual words.

This is the concept of the development of language, by combining three or four small words and creating a new word from them. And by doing this, providing us new definitions to address new challenges. Then, to create new words, there are three simple but important components: the root, the front, and the end portion.

Certain words, for example, hear, have just the root. Many other words, for instance, hearing, have both the root and also the end part. Yet others, like unheard, is made of the root and a front part. And while others, like unhearing, is made up of all three parts. So, how can this awareness enable you to understand odd words without looking at them? In a quite easy manner:

In fact, many of the major words which you are not aware of are composed of smaller words, in precisely the way we just mentioned. They are composed of the same three fundamental building blocks which we just discussed. Nevertheless, many of such smaller parts of the word are from Latin, for the very obvious fact that the Latin language was the old language, which was the mother of our present English language.

Consequently, what you need to do is study these Latin word sections and watch how they blend together to form new words, to figure out the definition of an odd word the first time you come across it.

Chapter 7:
Develop Massive Self-Confidence And Self-Esteem

Role of Confidence

Confidence is frequently associated with certainty. It is realizing and being mindful of your abilities and worth. Whenever you trust in your personal strength, judgement, and ability, you may claim that you are a confident individual.

Trust is not pride. You are not confident whenever you bring other individuals down to raise yourself up. In order to overstate your abilities, you are often not confident whenever you behave arrogantly.

Anytime your self-evaluation is similar to the facts, you have a strong level of confidence. Look out for the manner in which you act as it represents your trust level as well. Generally, confident individuals have a great posture, look others in the eye anytime they talk, and have a strong handshake and a simple and strong tone.

The Significance of Confidence

The importance of confidence is disregarded by some individuals. They are mistaken as confidence is a key part of life. In order to accomplish a lot of things, you require confidence, including achieving your personal goals. When there is no confidence, your chances of struggling are higher than your chances of winning.

Confidence really rates higher than physical beauty if we talk about attracting a partner. It was established by research published in the International Journal of Cosmetic Science that confidence reflects itself. Many male respondents participated in the research , and the individuals who used cologne displayed more confidence and pictured better.

In similar research published in the Journal of Personality and Social Psychology, it was discovered that anytime their female counterparts rank higher on the company hierarchy, men appeared to feel bad towards themselves.

When you wish to excel academically and personally, confidence is equally critical. Expert s have noticed that optimistic kids are more likely to turn into adults who are confident.

Excess confidence, however, is often advantageous. By carrying out research, experts from the University of California at San

Diego and the University of Edinburgh have proved this hypothesis. They also discovered that you have a greater chance of realizing your target despite lacking some skills or knowledge if you show confidence. You will thrive with excess confidence anytime you struggle for something that you really appreciate.

Even so, you need to be vigilant as well. While excess confidence can be beneficial, It could equally backfire. For instance, stop thinking positively but blindly. Overstating your skill can trigger you to be overloaded with assignments or inhibit your capacity to perform correctly.

What Follows Anytime Confidence is Lacking?

Indeed, self-confidence and self-esteem are far more critical than you would expect. In reality, they are essential for your cognitive performance. You would have a hard time combating complicated issues in life whenever you do not have an excellent level of self-worth. You will not have the capacity to make decisions and determine what you really like to become.

Essentially, the way you view yourself dictates how you fix the standard for how other individuals will see you. It'll reflect in your words and activities that you have confidence in yourself, and other individuals will believe in you as well. On the other hand, some other individuals will also begin to question your integrity if you don't have confidence in your own capacity.

The Buddhist monks conclude that low self-esteem is simply an illusion or a bad feeling that overstate one's constraints in terms of consistency, ability, and growth tendency. This implies that you will drop negatively and lose control over yourself when your self-confidence and self-esteem are very weak. You might start to perceive yourself as a victim that is unable to protect himself. You could also feel negligible, exempted, dejected, or overlooked. You might equally start to understand and accept other individual's criticism.

You need to be happy with whatever you have and have confidence in yourself when you wish to live a healthy and fulfilling life. You will not be delighted when you continuously try to satisfy others due to your low self-confidence and self-esteem. You've got the ability to change your life if you just know that.

How to Boost Your Confidence

So below are easy guidelines you can apply to enable you to get underway now that you have heard about confidence and the reason you have to develop it:

- Constantly Remind yourself that progress will inspire confidence.

You have discovered that it will make you happy in life to be a confident individual. Confidence will drive you to grow above your desired objective and succeed. Being good, nevertheless, will help you grow confident as well. It is similar to a circle event. Are you baffled?

Ok, just imagine it like this. You do not have the courage to speak to other individuals or battle for the things you need if you are cautious, nervous, and emotionally fragile. This can be a concern If you have to reach a better position in your selected sector. If you allow your coworkers to boss you about or are not able to say 'no' to those assignments, you may have a tough time receiving a promotion.

Nevertheless, you may still be good if you are intelligent and qualified enough. In your classroom, you will work tediously and be the best, enabling you to earn praise and appreciation. Because your report is higher than your colleagues', this equally places you at a massive advantage.

You will gain trust once you are successful. You know you're smart, and you've got your awards to support that assertion. As demonstrated by your designs, you recognize you are smart and experienced.

You should reflect back on your previous experiences if you have a period of sorrow or feel frustrated. To restore your mood, reflect on your accomplishments and prizes. Realizing that previously you have been successful will inspire you to do well, and you are able to succeed once again.

- To be successful, you should prepare yourself.

Most certainly, you have come across the adage that 'practice makes perfect.' Well, there is still some sense in that expression, despite that no single person is perfect. Practicing will hone your abilities and bring you closer to realizing your objectives.

To be a good individual, you should prepare yourself. You should get up very early in the day to work out, have a nice breakfast, and get ready for the daily routine. You should learn smarter rather than harder if you are still in school. You should try approaches that will enable you to do that.

Inspire yourself often if you are a sportsman who loses concentration and confidence. Learn and find ways of enhancing your concentration for long durations. Maintain a daily diary where your performance can be documented. This should enable you to recognise the weak spots and strengths that you have.

Another approach to preparing yourself to be a better individual is to formulate a method for setting your goals. It enables you to plan results and attains goals. Remember that planning is a vital factor for results and self-confidence. You can't depend solely on good fortune. For planned and unforeseen conditions, you have to be ready.

Plan your brain and body for both. However, do not exhaust yourself. You can actually start with smaller objectives. You can get frustrated when you set big initial targets, triggering your failure to achieve them. On the contrary, you develop a feeling of satisfaction if you meet smaller goals, which can inspire you to go on for bigger goals and targets.;

- Watch how other individuals succeed and strive to mimic what they do.

Finding a mentor is pretty straightforward. You will hear about the most influential individuals in your desired career.

For starters, you may get motivated by accomplished nurses if you're in medical school. You should do your study on them and create a chat with them, if feasible. Figure out the approach they applied in medical school to conquer challenges, thrive well in labs, and succeed. You may equally ask them about their practice as professional nurses.

You would need to follow the same methods and tactics by being able to determine with them. You recognize that the time they were younger, they encountered similar challenges as yours, and in spite, they somehow worked to make it to the top, so why won't you be able to do the same, right? You can be good also when you follow the path they have grazed. In fact, as you are already aware of the errors they have made, you can also accomplish greater feats, and you can stop doing them. You may also factor from your own experiences and knowledge learned.

- Give a pep talk to yourself.

The manner you perceive things and reason can be influenced greatly by your internal dialogue. Certainly, you ought to have a good internal dialogue if you wish to accomplish great stuff. If not, you will plunge downwards.

If you say to yourself repeatedly that you can achieve it, then you can certainly do it. On the opposite, you're not going to be motivated to do whatever you wish to do if you constantly doubt your ability and suggest that you can't.

Often, the narrow layer that divides hope and hopelessness is self-esteem and self-confidence. Even when you do not have the qualification, if you are only sufficiently optimistic, there is always a possibility for you to excel.

For instance, consider applying for a position, but you are not as qualified as the other candidates academically, you may either be intimidated or inspired to contend and outperform the better applicants by your lack of qualification.

You could be the person selected for the role if you convince the employer that you are a far better choice. Therefore, you have to stand firm, talk plainly, and with confidence. This manner, as a person who is qualified, intelligent, and willing, you may sell yourself perfectly.

- Act confidently

Your feelings, opinions, and attitudes are all intertwined. Each influences the other. Whatever you think affects the way you feel, which essentially reflects in your actions and speech.

You may render yourself uncomfortable anytime you give yourself bad internal dialogue. Due to this, you can get anxious and display stress. As an indicator of anxiety, you can begin to stammer and wander back and forth.

You may equally begin to think of all the stuff that may go wrong rather than the stuff you should do well. It just makes you get overwhelmed by getting a negative outlook on life, compromising the likelihood of thriving in your activities.

Nevertheless, if you behave with confidence, you may overcome your anxiety and pull things off. Say you're aiming for your company's head and are about to make a speech right in front of all the stakeholders, but you're not really the brightest or the most skilled. What are you going to do? Do you let them know that you're flawed? That might cause them to doubt your skills and not entrust you with enormous duties. Some others may lose some regard for you, also.

Show everybody you have what it requires to become the head if you wish to succeed. Talk and behave with utmost confidence. When you speak, look everyone straight in the eye. Try to have a great handshake, hold your back straight, keep your head up, and prevent twitching.

And if you are consumed with fear inside, on the outside, you could still hide it. You will finally make yourself believe you are fully confident. This will impact other people's opinion of you, and they will equally think you are competent and deserving of their vote.

- Ascertain and keep your power pose for two minutes.

Harvard University associate professor and social psychologist Amy Cuddy performed research on high and low power poses to assess their impact on applicants during work interviews.

The research respondents were split into two classes. While a group was asked to try the low power poses, the other category was asked to try the high power poses. The people who tried the high power poses were discovered to outperform those individuals who tried the ow power poses.

They were capable of taking on greater risks, which changed their physiology greatly. In summary, greater testosterone and reduced cortisol levels were correlated with high-power poses.

Via high power poses, you, as well, may change your physiology considerably. You may try the superhero pose, for example. Mimic the Superman pose. Stand firm, loosen your back, and stay aligned with your shoulders. Keep your head up, place your hands against your waist, and put your legs apart.

Feel the force flowing around your body as you remain in this position. When drawing deep breaths, keep the stance for two minutes. When you are on the verge of doing something that surprises you, try this stance. It's going to inspire you and restore your confidence again.

- Get the future visualized.

Although being aware of your current state is more essential than feeling negative about your experience and thinking about your future, don't ignore the role of planning and goal-setting. Besides, y our current state is a step into your future. You may put things in a positive light by getting a future view of yourself. You will be more economically accountable for your retirement and begin saving some money. In order to secure a good job and develop a career, you would be more inspired to pursue your education more seriously.

Don't worry about the long-term, but don't neglect it entirely. What you need to do is stay calm and make fair choices. Two distinct aspects are being nervous and being organized.

Anytime you feel worried about the future, bad thoughts are what you visualize. You expect events that eventually take a wrong turn. Nevertheless, as you prepare yourself, remain optimistic that things will reverse for the better. It will enable you to make great decisions and be more effective in life by getting such positive ideas.

Chapter 8:
Retention And Comprehension Skill

Conducive Learning Environments

- **How can we learn?**

It appears like such a straightforward question, but several years of empirical literature seem not to agree with that opinion. We can only assume learning as an exercise that we just began as an infant with no planning. We were the repository for a steady influx of knowledge and ideas throughout our school days. And teachers assessed how much we learned in most conventional environments by replicating the data back to them. We didn't have a choice then and basically followed what had been given to us.

This gathering and reiteration of knowledge somewhat suggest that learning is a subconscious act that can only be supervised, not managed. In reality, there are variables, weaknesses, and circumstances that influence our capacity to learn. Knowing these components will enable you to prevent errors and speed up your learning process. This section offers concepts and strategies of science that will enable you to understand in a manner that applies best to you.

Both mental behaviors are affected by internal and extraneous influences and circumstances, even learning. Some variables that we can regulate; others that we have to tackle or maneuver around. The empirical concepts that guide our learning skills and many of the good strategies we can apply to improve learning ability are addressed in this chapter. In other words, we have to establish productive environments for learning; else, we are trying to sabotage ourselves.

You're not going to attempt to learn to ski in the desert, are you?

Learning in Blocks of Short Time

We offer sufficient body time to refresh and reinvigorate and encourage us to hold more details over extended durations by dividing our learning plans into blocks of time. Consequently, beginning a fresh learning schedule by basically planning a schedule is a great idea.

- Long-term scheduling.

Plan out your timetable to organize a learning routine at the start of a course, class, or technical project. You can effectively do this using a free web calendar application from nearly all Internet providers or on a print calendar or worksheet.

Many of us begin the day in high-productive mode, whereas others are typically nocturnal creatures, thinking which times of day you prefer to get the most achieved. Simply make sure you leave enough sleeping and eating time. In reality, there is an empirical justification, summarized by the words morning larks and night owls, for if you are the type that is more alert at night time or in the day time.

When you're actually plugged into your brain and mind, by adding the 90-minute pattern to the schedule, for example, 90-minute blocks of time that account for rests and exhaustion, you can become a little more robust with your planning. This needs a bit more thorough self-reflection and tracking, though you may fine-tune your learning plan even more when you are able to narrow down an even more precise moment when your learning skills are better.

- Blocks for learning.

You may change the 30-50-minute learning session as determined by the LSU report for your personal reasons. Recall that 30 minutes is adequate to render the learning session important enough, and that is going over 50 places unnecessary stress on your brain. So, be sure to arrange a counterpart break at the end of your key learning period during your weekly block of time.

Also, adapt it to something you are sure your brain can handle: perhaps a 10-minute break for 50 minutes time or a 15-minute break for 45 minutes study time, feel free. If needed, the learning session will go all the way down to 30 minutes. The famous Pomodoro clock, widely employed for work efficiency, may be applied for 25 minutes of operation then accompanied by five minutes of complete withdrawal from that activity. It's not difficult and simple to set a particular period of time. It simply has to be a time frame convenient enough for you to work with on a routine basis.

Simply ask yourself the way you could appeal to a jellyfish or maybe a child's attention span. Our mature brains are not so different as we would like to imagine.

Memory Retention

Absolutely, our memory is strongly linked to learning. If memory is a reservoir mechanism that resides within particular brain connections, then attempting to adapt one's actions and thought to the introduction of new knowledge is about modifying brain connections. They rely on each other since the purpose of learning is to absorb new information into the memory, and without the opportunity to learn more, our memory is worthless.

Memorization is the way we preserve and retrieve knowledge for use (basically the learning process), and the construction of memory takes 3 phases. A mistake in either of these phases will lead to information that is not translated to memory adequately, a poor memory or the sensation of "I may not be able to recall his name, though he was putting on purple."

- Encoding
- Storage
- Retrieval

The stage of interpreting information via your senses is encoding. We regularly find ourselves doing this, and even right now, you are doing it. Via most of your senses, you encode knowledge both deliberately and inadvertently. If you study a text, you use your eyes to encode the details, but what magnitude of focus and attention do you really use? Otherwise, it may be argued that you instinctively encode data, such as listening to songs at a cafeteria or watching cars pass you by right in red light traffic, the more time and concentration you dedicate to a task, the more aware your encoding gets.

How much concentration and time you spend often shows how effective the memory is and, therefore, whether that information just gets to your short attention span or whether it goes via the channel to your long-term memory. The encoding is usually not so deep or heavy when you are studying a book as you watch the television.

Storage would be the next move once you have learned and encoded the details with your senses. Once it goes via your eyes or ears, what becomes of this information? There are usually three possibilities for where this data should move to, and they decide if there is a memory you may consciously be aware of existing.

Three memory mechanisms basically exist:

- Sensory memory,
- Short-term memory, and
- Long-term memory.

Retrieval is the final stage in the memory system. It is time we finally utilize our minds and can be assumed to have remembered something. Maybe you can remember it from nothing, or maybe you require a prompt to pull up the memory. Some memories can solely be memorized together or as part of an entity, such as memorizing the ABCs and then remembering that you have to say it to recall the way it works. Typically, whatever the attention you have provided to the information storage and encoding processes, defines how simple it is to recover such information. Much of the learning activity is not necessarily based on rehabilitation, focusing on the storage component and the things you may try to force memories into long-term regions from sensory and short-term regions.

Think of the time you're cramming for an exam. You wish that the information that you perceive for maybe 48 hours to be in your memory; that implies that it must live past short-term memory and probably beyond sensory memory. You may not even care if you recall this knowledge about the subject matter at the end of the year, so you will hit a degree of concentration and focus that will drive the details between short-term and long-term memory right into the cloudy area. In fact, what's going on is that you're going to rehearse the details sufficiently to give your long-term memory a rather slight impression.

In a way, speeding up your learning is similar to enhancing your memory ability and the degree of how retentive your memory is—the more porous, the greater.

Forgetting

Training, though, is both the method of developing memory while still making it easier not to forget. Why are we forgetting? Why can't we recall this reality? How did we ever let anything skip our minds?

Forgetting is typically a flaw or weakness in the storage phase, as you have heard. The details you desire just reach the short-term, not the long-term memory. The issue is not that you cannot locate the details in your mind; it's that to start with, the detail wasn't rooted deeply enough in your brain.

It's simpler atimes to think of forgetting as a studying mistake. Typically, you recover or access your memory in three major ways:

- Recall
- Recognition
- Re-learning

Recalling is when you recollect information without external signals. This is the moment you can pronounce something in a void room on command, such as staring at a small sheet of paper and then putting down the capitals of all of the world's nations. You have the best memories of it when you can remember stuff. You have either practiced it sufficiently or added ample meaning to it so that it becomes extremely powerful information inside your long-term memory. Absolutely, since recall reflects the highest degree of memory, it is also generally the hardest to accomplish. To reach a level close to this, it would usually take hours of practice or analysis. We like details to reach this level anytime we read, but we will normally compromise for the next form of memory retrieval.

Recognition is anytime you are able to conjure up your brain in light of an outside cue. It's anytime you may not have the capacity to recall anything through mere recall, though if you have a little hint or reminder, you'll be able to recollect it. You may not have the capacity to recall all the capitals of the countries of the world, for instance, but if you had a hint like the capital's first alphabet or anything that flows with the capital, it'd be pretty simple to remember it. This is usually how we end up anytime we cram information. This is the manner mnemonics, and related memory devices apply as well. We understand that with a large degree of practice, we cannot retain and remember too many bits of information confidently.

As a result, we focus on stacking data into easily identifiable signs.

Relearning is the worst method of retrieval, undeniably. It happens anytime you relearn or revisit data, and every successive time, it requires you lesser effort. When you study a collection of nation capitals on Wednesday, for instance, and it lasts you 40 minutes, the following day could last you 20 minutes, and so on. Sadly, this is how we mainly lie on a regular basis. We may be acquainted with a definition, but by the time we look at it once more, we haven't really registered enough of it into the memory to prevent basically relearning it. This is exactly what arises anytime we are unfamiliar with a subject, or we have actually forgotten much of it. You have basically not stored anything beyond the threshold of short-term memory into long-term memory while you are in the relearning period.

Strategies for Active Learning

In 2013, expert John Dunlosky and his colleagues performed a detailed analysis of learning-related methods and models. They tested ten different approaches, selected as they were "comparatively simple to apply and could therefore be embraced by many students." You would possibly recognize all of them as strategies you have used in the past with different effectiveness levels. The team of Dunlosky assessed each approach in line with how well they were tailored to the purpose of learning and retention. As could be predicted, the five approaches that the team assumed were bad for learning proved to be, undoubtedly, the most widely adopted and accepted:

- Summarization

Students, in this approach, are required to compose their own document summaries to be studied. The purpose of the summary is to "locate and convey the essence of a document's key ideas while neglecting irrelevant or redundant content." Dunlosky's team believed that summary is an ability that solely applies when the student is previously trained in the manner to do it. The strategy could not be performed and would not be successful for most of the students with no previous instruction. In other words, this could be productive, and on paper it is, but you are possibly doing it incorrectly.

- Highlighting

This famous, widely used approach consists of labeling or underscoring relevant ideas with a colorful ink marker. These experts discovered that if students used it on an extremely complicated text, highlighting could benefit a little, but generally, they regard highlighting as a diversion from learning because it does not enable students to derive extra sense or conclusion from the learning content.

- Mnemonics

Mnemonics is a virtually primitive activity, the use of cognitive references or symbolic pictures, poems, words, or abbreviations to remember details or knowledge previously known, such as applying the term "Super Man Helps Everyone" to recognize the Great Lakes (Superior, Michigan, Huron, Erie, Ontario) or employing pictures of items to learn a new language. Expert s discovered that while it can enable us to reach keyword memory easily, the ability to achieve "quality learning" from mnemonics was very limited. This may be linked to the connection between rote learning and theory learning.

- Usage of imagery for text learning.

This system inspires students to evoke a picture, mentally or on print, to depict passages or pieces of content that they learn, a more conceptual application of mental induction than mnemonics. The experts discovered this application of imagery "effective," although further study was required on the subject. To sum up, they discovered that the advantages of using imagery were restricted to cognitive tests and content that previously lent itself to making or remembering images.

- Re-reading

Dunlosky's team noticed that while rereading and evaluating text was incredibly popular and easy to conduct, it was only relatively successful and majorly when rereading of the content was spaced apart. They further stated that there was no convincing proof that rereading had any impact on the awareness, skills, or deep understanding of the subject by students.

Although these five strategies were not without their benefits, either their simplicity of application or their efficacy anytime students learned the way to apply them properly, Dunlosky discovered their usefulness in preserving somewhat limited thorough knowledge, comprehensiveness, and relevance and sometimes subject to certain circumstances. . They retained some importance in superficial significance or memorization, but much less in understanding.

Chapter 9:
Develop A Photographic Memory And Improvement

The Peg or Rhyme Method

The time you were a child, do you recall learning childhood rhymes and music? It's no accident that we're teaching young children stuff that is simple to recall. When you eventually become an adult, Rhyme can appear dumb, but your memory still maintains this sort of data far more effectively. Song lines, phrases, and verses that rhyme are still far simpler to recall than any old daily script for us "big kids."

Ok, we will be using this cognitive ability to make the most out of it adapt it to our brain. Let me guide you little by little through this easy but very significant and valuable activity. The strategy has been in existence for a very long time. In the 1600s, Henry Herdson was recognized for this invention.

This activity is generally quite simple for auditory learners, though anyone can learn it quickly because of its simplicity. It basically needs 10 minutes of your time, so kindly don't simply read it. Learn to work with it!

Step 1

Memorize and try to replicate these ten items in sequence. You've got 2 minutes.

List to be Memorized:

- Duck
- Movie
- Goat
- Frog
- Goggles
- Helmet
- Ladder
- Robots
- Owl
- Golden Rock

Step 2

How many of them were you able to memorize correctly? Now close the item without looking at the item again and answer the below question. Which object occupied the three-place? 8? 10? Hold on, and check how many of the objects you could remember correctly.

Step 3

Memorize the following figures together with the words that sound in harmony with them. This is going to be much simpler than the former exercise.

- Sun
- Blue
- Tree
- Door
- Dive
- Bricks
- Heaven
- Date
- Wine
- Zen

Return back to the initial list after memorizing the number of rhythmic pairs and constructing a vibrant picture for every one of the items.

For instance: One-Sun-Duck, duck is the first thing on the list that you attempt to memorize when aligning it with first, please. You may generate a vibrant picture of a duck heading into the sunset. For the rest of the pictures, try this.

Step 4

After you have successfully memorized the pairs above, note the items in sequence.

Step 5

Can we repeat the former workout but modify the sequence?

Step 6

Hold on until the following day to see how many things you are able to remember in order. Do this again within a week. You'll be shocked by what your mind is capable of doing.

Memory Palace or Loci Approach to Recall

The Memory Palace is often referred to as Loci's Method. It is a transition theory of a known physical position. Reflect back into your infancy home, the house of a mate, your holiday residence, or your middle school. Possibilities are, you're will be able to do a cognitive replay of places that you normally visit. In reality, humans have been recognized as so-called geospatial gurus.

The background underlying the word "palace of memory" originates from Old Greece. Nevertheless, its logical reliability has been challenged, making it a great story. Simonides Ceosxv (c. 546 - 486 BCE) gave a speech at a feast in ancient Greece.

For a certain reason, he was summoned outside, and at that instance, the building fell, and everybody right inside perished.

By psychologically restoring the feast and marking the remains of the dead, Simonides is said to have been able to give relief to the relatives of the people based on where he recalled their respective position.

Important: Memory is never an image. It's revolutionary. The better you are able to make your mental picture vibrant, wild, loud, and insane, the better you can recall events and their pattern.

In the beginning, it may appear dumb, but you don't have to inform everyone what strategies you're using. Only if you want to share, the external world may not see the innovation side.

Note: Your walkthrough of your preferred Memory Palace ought to engage all senses in order to be efficient:

- Sight
- Sound
- Touch
- Taste
- Smell.

The more vibrant the pictures you are able to make, the more you are able to recall. The purpose you recall clear memories that is distinct from the remaining is termed the Isolation Effect, invented by the German psychiatrist Hedwig Von Restorffxvi, sometimes regarded as the Von Restorff Effect. She found that when many homogeneous products/stimuli are involved, the distinct one is more likely to be remembered.

Develop Your Personal Memory Palace

Let us create many of your individual Memory Palace. It doesn't need to be a real palace. Any structure that you know the inside architecture and can do a comprehensive psychological walk-through would do. Choose a place, preferably If it's a residence or apartment common to you. You will build a range of Memory Palaces and ensure that they are chosen according to the size and difficulty as appropriate to the list or number you are trying to memorize.

Memory Palaces ideas:

- Your infancy residence
- Your present home
- Your school hostel
- Your workplace
- Your middle school or University campus
- The grocery shop in the suburb
- A shopping mall you regularly visit
- The gym centre
- Your colleague's house
- The cruise ship you visited on holiday

Essentially, whatever place that you feel relaxed and understand your surroundings will function as a Memory Palace. The probability is that you can quickly come up with a minimum of 20 Memory Palaces. Try a cognitive flashback and shut your eyes. Even when you haven't visited a location in over 25 years, you can quickly recall going from room to room, if it was familiar to you in the past.

As people, this is one of the rare abilities that we have. We have a knack for recalling places. Choose a selection of places, from big to small, so you can match your collections and numbers. For instance, if you need to memorize a large set of numbers, choose something larger than a studio apartment.

Brain Tips to Note

- **Exercise**

Sometimes a young man at the workplace was told by an incredibly smart and sophisticated colleague of mine that she did not exercise as it was not an educational practice. "In her absence, the man stated, "Well, when you are not able to exercise, you're going to have about 12 years less productive work to do in life. Average? Yeah, sort of... But that's real as well.

The human body is a comprehensive system. Your mind could have roles that are distinct, but it is not an organ separate from the body. The brain benefits from exercise as it decreases insulin sensitivity and disease. Increasing mood and rest is equally a great advantage, which is a strategy in enhancing mental performance.

- **Reduce sugar and refined food consumption.**

A meal with excessive sugar and processed foods is harmful to the memory. The human body is a comprehensive system. Fast food is not only going to your gut. Common sense shows that the toxins will circulate all over your body, even though the blood-brain barrier. Anything that will make your body sick and obese has the power to make your brain sick is as well. Feeding garbage into your body equally means loading shit in your brain.

- **Doodle**

Whenever you are in a boring team talk or meetings, a study has revealed that anytime your mind moves without purpose, you do not pay attention, so you do not retain details. On the contrary, you can always concentrate on whatever is being conveyed while you are doodling. This is what I have tried on several occasions, and it helps!

Doodling prevents your brain from fantasising. Your mind will still work intently and remember details if you draw or paint something. You are basically concentrating your attention by keeping your hands occupied. Therefore, if you're the leader running a conference, give those that doodle a break as you speak. They're likely to show more interest than the fantasists.

- **Play word games**

In the modern environment, anytime machines and smartphones execute a load of mental programming for us, we attribute it to our mind to hold it in shape. In order to consolidate long-term experiences, we have spoken in length about the role of regular retrieval. Word games are a perfect way to achieve that.

- **Repeat and Recall**

I feel it is safe to assume that many of us, either on TV or the internet, have witnessed our good share of commercials.

Even if I have not seen them in several years, I can imitate many advertising bylines from my infancy. With time, repetition has a compounding impact.

This is actually the uniqueness of advertising. You may not purchase instantly, but since it establishes a trend, which in turn improves trust, you can be convinced with time. Repetition actually supports the memory but works the most if merged with vivid visual imagery.

- **Using Visualization**

The effective way to recall is to imagine using all your senses while you are listening to a voice note or program. Your mind is struck regularly with a lot of information that it needs to dismiss a large part of it as irrelevant background sound to work.

Choose the things you like to recall, make a vibrant, insane picture out of it that is unique and you can remember.

- **Develop stories to recall.**

Stories are the way we recall several historical and empirical principles (think of Newton's Laws of Motion). Stories are at the core of the manner we perceive and interact. Our brains adapt to stories much easier than just random lists.

- **Avoid multitasking**

I was once a great multitasker, but it is not necessarily a perfect way to be effective, as studies show. It is very easy to become distracted by cat/dog images, office messages, news headlines, that we easily lose concentration on the things we were working on initially.

Effectively use muscle memory (aka motor learning)! Note the adage "It's like riding a bike."?? A lot of things can be learned, like:

- Play your musical instrument
- Learn to type quicker,
- Learn Martial Arts
- Dance
- Create Art

Food is Medicine

You might be wondering why we are talking about diets in a book on memory improvement? If you munch fries or consume a raw vegan meal, this book's methods will work effectively.

Nevertheless, as with good sleep and a balanced diet, human beings seem to focus more effectively and function more effectively. Consuming more vegetables solely won't teach you the strategy, though it will make you feel better and focus more so that you can devote more attention to the job at hand. I'm still puzzled by the way many doctors only discuss consuming a plant-based diet often (or entirely) as a reconsideration or not at all.

Doctors and others in the healthcare profession usually prefer to be compensated on a service fee system. Can you remember the last time your doctor earned financial benefits just the time you got stronger or for disease prevention? This is a big concern with our medical service. We are also disease-centric rather than concentrating more on control.

Food is medicine, though it may equally be poison, based on the things you eat.

Genetics has its function

Human beings in harsh weather such as drought and near the Arctic have adapted genetically to conform to some diets just to survive.

Many individuals desire a fast remedy, a pill for a miracle. You may check the advantages of a plant-based meal by beginning to introduce one plant-based diet at a time, even when you hail from a chronic meatatarian family like I am. Assess for yourself, and see the way you feel.

I deem myself as a "cheagan," a deceptive vegan, just not there yet, though my whole day is unique anytime I only consume plant-based dishes. When we talk about being mentally bright and conscious, there is never a brain fog that makes a really huge difference.

Having said that, I learned the tough way that if you strive to follow it in certain nations where water is polluted, a raw food vegan meal can have certain very severe bad effects such that anything as basic as a raw salad can put you in the clinic for infectious disease. Look for a balance. We are already aware that trash and refined foods, particularly added sugar = bad, vegetables = good. This is a tutorial on memory strategies and not a diet program, but the memory is also influenced by the things you feed into your belly.

You will not purchase an exotic car and use inferior fuel to fill it up, will you? Likewise, your brain. It needs the greatest ever fuel. I see myself as a "cheagan," a manipulative vegan.

Chapter 10:
Skills To Remember Quicker

How to Turn Words to Images

The Audionym

"Audio" implies sound. "Nym" stands for the name. For any word you wish to recall, an audionym is an audio name (a soundalike). It is vital to know that auditory symbols are centered on sound and not spelling.

An audionym for every word can be generated. Note, the audionym should be something that the word you wish to recall sounds like (or maybe suggests) and should be something you are able to see. Examples of audionyms I produced for a variety of subjects are below:

State	Audionym
Pennsylvania	Pencil
Tennessee	Tennis (racquet or ball)
Montana	Mountain
Delaware	Deli
Iowa	Eye (soundalike, not spelling)

Country	Audionym
Netherlands	Net
Canada	Can
Brazil	Bracelet
Bulgaria	Bull
BOLIVIA	Bowl

Chemicals Element	Audionym
Hydrogen	Hydrant
Helium	Heel
Boron	Boar
Carbon	Car
Nitrogen	Knight

Planet	Audionym
Mercury	Marker
Earth	Ear
Jupiter	Juice
Neptune	Napkin
Pluto	Plate

You will acquire an outstanding knowledge of the audionym system by studying the above terms and their proposed audionyms.

How to Develop Audionyms

Word	Audionym
Pennsylvania	Pencil
Jackson	Jack
April	Ape

You can't see Pennsylvania, Jackson, or April, however, you are able to see a pencil, a jack, or an ape. The aim of the audionym is essential to translate details you wish to study into items that you are able to see that are soundalike.

The name Pennsylvania does not actually inform you of the word pencil. Nevertheless, anytime you are handling the topic states, and pencil is the audionym, Pennsylvania would automatically spring to your mind. Audionym would be one of the memory resources you apply most often.

Some phrases indicate clear auditory symbols. Instantly, they indicate an object that you can see. If you wish to remember China, the nation, you can imagine China, the dinnerware. Suppose the tone of the first syllable(s) of the word to recall automatically suggests(s) an entity you are acquainted with. In that case, other words seem obvious: Canada, Poland, Belgium, organisation, etc. Other terms still don't imply something instantly. Examples of this include Mexico, confidence, and purpose. To construct audionyms, these terms need a bit more thought. A few tips are listed here:

Word	Audionym
Mexico	Mixer
Confidence	Confetti
Purpose	Porpoise

Say the word quickly to see whether it gives a soundalike entity to mind as you get to a word that you require an audionym for. Then say it gently. What item do you think it sounds like? Note, it is the manner in which the word sounds, not the way it is pronounced, that counts. Bear in mind, though, that the audio should be something you are able to see. Audionyms can start to come to mind very readily with only a little practice.

Here are some further examples of last name auditonyms. Remember that they are past presidents' last names, too.

Name	Audionym
Ford	Ford (vehicle)
Van Buren	Van
Carter	Cart
Eisenhower	Eyes
Hayes	Hay
Cleveland	Cleaver

A Ford is already an item you can imagine, as you can see in the earlier cases. The first syllable might indicate a car or a cart in the Carter name; I'd use a cart since it is very similar to the Carter name. The name 'Eisenhower' in the first syllable is not pronounced like eyes, though it sounds similar to eyes. That renders eyes a great audionym for Eisenhower.

Tips for Developing Audionyms

- Do not build an audionym for a word only if you know the way to say the word.
- Audionym should be a sound-like entity that can be visualized.
- The object or idea you are working on should be familiar to you.
- For every syllable in the term that you like to recall, you don't need to construct an audionym. To prompt the answer for you, the audionym will reflect just enough of the starting of the term. Pen, for instance, implies Pennsylvania (or pencil implies Pennsylvania). When the detail is not explicit enough when examining the content, supplementary syllables may require audionyms to offer you the proper answer.
- Say the term quick or sluggish when you have trouble developing an audionym for a term.

- It doesn't need to sound precisely like the term that you like to recall. Your natural memory and intuition would be of help.
- It's not enough for audionyms to simply rhyme with the term you wish to recall. An audionym must have equivalent, or very close, consonant sounds.

The audionym is as essential to my learning approach as the letter is to the written word. Amazingly, you recall more of the things you see than the things you hear or read. The audionym becomes an image of the details you wish to recall.

The secret to your growth in improving your memory capacity would be your ability to alter what you hear or read into audionyms. Please do not get frustrated when it takes some time to build audionyms at first. The more you try it, the clearer it will get.

How to Remember by Association

One visual item's connection with another in a certain illogical manner is the next stage in the learning process. It is definitely not unusual to use associations to recall items. This approach was applied very well by ancient scholars.

It is fascinating to see the way "memory by association" is well understood by certain individuals. I once spoke to a group of around 500 and only remembered a 100-digit number provided to me in collections of two figures simultaneously. I hadn't even seen the figures. Only once had I experienced each collection. After recalling the 100 digits correctly, I heard somebody say, 'I wonder the way he did it. It's all by association." Absolutely, he was correct, but what did I associate with what?" The approach ought to be more than mere association in order to function. It has to be straightforward, powerful, quick, and simple. Below are a few essential things to note about the method of association:

Often begin the connection with the things you'll know later. For instance, you'll know the state in which you wish to remember the capital city. You'll know the face that you wish to remember the name. You'll know the individual you like to remember, the cell number, and so on.

It still makes the association so irrational that in practical situations it will never arise. This could take some time at first, as you may not be used to thinking fallaciously.

Irrespective of how complicated the information is that you wish to understand and recall, any association will require just two items simultaneously. Much like you did the time you saw the nine items for the first nine leaders in the previous example, nothing you learn would be more complicated than associating two items together in an irrational manner.

How to Develop Powerful Associations

It is hard to persuade individuals that a well-structured memory is never something with which someone is born. Memory practice does not differ from any other acquired ability. There are some mechanisms and a level of mental flexibility to be followed that grows with training. There are just three ways we can recall, apart from hypnosis and electronic or chemical activation of cells in the brain:

- **Repetition**

This has usually been the extremely popular learning approach as it is the major technique many individuals are acquainted with. Strategies of structured memory are not well recognized. It is time demanding and costly to learn by repetition. In order to be preserved, knowledge gathered by repetition should be continuously replicated. In reality, forgetting begins immediately repetition ends. Repetition is the least effective form of learning, irrespective of what learning type is applied (visual, auditory, kinesthetic, and so forth). Is it not surprising that, in our formal education, the least successful learning technique is the most prevalent teaching technique?

- **Impression**

This technique is effective, though it is the least realistic since, by impression, we do not have the chance to decide the things we can remember. Memory by impression happens anytime we undergo a terrifying event, such as something that leaves our brains with an effect or impression that we couldn't erase it even though we tried.

- **Association**

This means associating the things you like to recall with the things you already know, irrationally. This is, without a doubt , very much better compared to any other technique for remembering. Firstly, your innate ability to recall the things you see is capitalized on. Secondly, objects that are irrational, excessive in volume or number, or out-of-proportion are simpler to recall.

As they reach the stage of our senses, the written words we study and the spoken words we hear generally have no images. I assume that individuals who have strong, powerful memories are individuals who subconsciously see images of words spoken or written. There is no question that certain images flash through their heads, allowing them to maintain data stronger than the average individual. Nevertheless, many of us are usually not in that group. Therefore, we ought to train ourselves to structure the knowledge we like to recall by applying for memory programs. These help us see the details that we hear and read and cement it into our minds.

If carefully structured, the association strategy involves two essential components: "the things you know already" and "the things you like to recall." For instance, there are four essential components to be associated with any time you're meeting an individual for the very first time: the person's name and his face. You would already know the individual's face at any future time whenever you like to remember the name.

Did you ever hear anyone say, "I can recall your face, but I apologise. I simply can't recall your name." You sure did! Although, did you ever hear someone say, "Hello, Joe," or "Hello, Sally, I remember your name. However, I can't remember your face?" No! That really doesn't happen! And you know what you actually saw, you see the face, and you recall it. You hear the word, and you forget it as you forget the things you hear.

Any association has to start with the things you know. For instance, if you like to recall your colleague John's cell number, you will not associate John with the cell number. You'd associate the cell number with John. In this situation, John is what you know (as you will know that it is John whom you like to call). What you like to recall is the cell number. "You're never going to think, "This is the phone number I like to dial. Who owns the number? You'd think, rather, "I like to call John, what's his number?" "

You have to determine the things you will know anytime you have to recall it to make an efficient association between any two things, then associate whatever you like to recall with what you will know. You will learn to consistently keep records in your memory via the influence of association and recall it with amazing precision. For the moment, it is crucial that you recall starting any association with it (whatever that you are sure you will know whenever it is time to remember the information being mentally stored).

Rules for Developing Association

- Define the "known" (the things you will know at the time you like to remember the information) and convert it to an audionym (a soundalike that you can see). If the known is in the numerical list or is a physical place, since you can see it already, you don't construct an audionym.
- Define and convert the details you like to recall to an audionym.
- Picture the known audionym in its regular position (or a physical position in its usual place).
- Associate the details you like to recall with the known position or audionym.
- Whenever you're making the association, be sure that it is so odd, absurd, funny, irrational, or out-of-proportion that in practical life, it will not happen.

- Multiply the data Audionym. By analyzing the data audionym multiplied by thousands and sometimes millions, the association will typically be reinforced.
- To improve your association, apply the whole of your senses, if possible. Embed yourself in this irrational association. S ee it! Hear that! Just feel it! Smell that! Taste it!
- The further you are able to integrate action into your association, the simpler it will be to recall.
- Individual involvement. Engage yourself in your associations, where necessary. It can have more of an impact on your memory when it's you that is involved.
- As a basic guideline, it is not irrational enough when the association is feasible in actual situations.

You will still be clear about the defined audionym or physical position. They feature in the bold form in the below examples:

- Seeing a **face** and trying to recall the name.
- Anytime you like to call a **person** or a **location** and need the number.
- Whenever you need your **car keys**, or **sunglasses**, or **something else**, and you ponder where you kept them.
- You conceive a **state,** and you want to recall its capital city.

- If you conceive the **novel title** and want to recall its name.
- When you're thinking about a **meal** and like to determine the calories.
- If you think about a **motion picture** and want the actors and actresses to be remembered.

The rules for developing irrational associations are clear. However, before they become "a part of living," you should learn and implement these guidelines. Association is by far the most fundamental and certainly among the most essential strategies of all memory.

Before you use it to a piece of particular information, it is important to understand the manner the association strategy functions. Before adding the notes to a particular song, it's kind of like studying each note on the musical scale.

Chapter 11:
Increase Memory Productivity

How Powerful Is Your Memory?

The odds are that it is still in pretty decent condition, whether you believe your memory is poor or doing relatively good. It's possible, however, that nobody has taught you the way to activate its real potential. When you become aware that you cannot remember people's names, the place you dropped your phone, or the new password for your internet banking app, self-doubt might have crept in.

The following strategies will help you develop a strong and productive memory. Write down your responses and keep track in the notebook of your ratings.

Observation and Visualization

I want you to visualize or imagine different objects, faces, and locations. Many individuals feel that since they do not create a faithful depiction of objects, such as almond or dog, in their mind's eye, then these strategies will not be effective. Nevertheless, a photographic reproduction of the object does not have to be produced: all that is needed is merely to picture some especially memorable feature of the object you are trying to envision.

Let's say there's a sabertooth tiger you like to imagine. There is no point in imagining the exact dimensions of its teeth. In regards to its head or the sun's glint hitting its hair. Only picture a cartoon object with black eyes and perhaps some powerful jaws of a large black and fluffy white cat.

I notice that I focus on having a flash of one aspect of the item as I hunt through a list of, say, 200 words and attempt to commit them to memory. For instance, all I can picture is a shoelace for the word shoe or a telephone. I could get a swift image of the keypad on my phone.

Note, not only can the word "imagine" mean to shape a mental picture, it can equally mean to concoct or invent. The picture you construct is unique to you, it solely exists in your memory, and beyond this vision, it is not genuine.

There are strategies for improving mental imaging abilities, and the more you engage your memory, the better your internal eye will get.

Activity: Observational Visualisation

This is a perfect activity to strengthen your memory's visual aspect and grow observational powers.

- Firstly, get hold of any household item, such as a smartphone, flower pot, flask, or radio. Let's say you pick your flask: explore as many parts of it as possible and analyze it for around 25 to 30 seconds.

- Cover your eyes after that and try and remember as many parts of the object as you could in your mind's eye. To start with, all you can remember is the design of the body of the flask and the design of the handle. Open your eyes at any point you run out of ideas and gather more information, such as the design of the nozzle or the label of the maker.
- Cover your eyes once again and connect your initial mental image to your latest observations. After that, open your eyes to see more detail about the about. Continue to repeat this sequence of opening your eyes-observe-close eyes-examine until you have processed as many characteristics of the flask as you can.
- Then, try to draw these memorized characteristics in your journal without staring at the item. If your visualized memories of the flask are depleted, take one last look to observe if there is any more information that you might add to your preserved mental image log.

The Body System

In this phase, I will provide you with an expedient memory system for those times when you like to take in something instantly. The Body System is a rather easy but powerful approach to store a few things, such as a grocery list. It works by integrating body parts with the main creative mental images of the object you would like to recall. The more evocative or enhanced the image, the better, as this will enable you to fix it in your mind. With this method, there seem to be no clear and strict rules. However, I would recommend that you restrict it to storing not more than ten objects. From your head down to your feet, or vice versa, you may work through a list.

Let us assume that the following 10-item shopping list needs to be remembered: blue paint, dog biscuits, newspaper, lantern, medicine, chicken, toothpaste, bananas, batteries for shampoos, and alarm clocks.

I have a picture of myself putting my leg in an open container of blue paint. I can picture a dog jumping up to my knee. A flattened newspaper comes out of my wallet (thigh). A ray of light is glowing from my belly button. There's a prescription fixed to my chest. A sheep is sitting behind my back. I'm smearing toothpaste around my mouth. My nose is banana-shaped. My hair is wrapped in a froth of shampoo. I have a loud, buzzing alarm clock in my hand.

With a little creativity, I can easily memorize a list of things.

The Link Method

The Link Method is an easy and efficient way for any to memorize data series, whether a checklist or a collection of names, ideas, items, instructions, etc. An unleashing of innovative thinking is all that is needed.

How do you use the Link Method to recall the four things, hand, butter, magnet, and atlas, in series? Assume dipping your hand in some butter. You detach an adhesive magnet from the inside of the butter. The magnet draws you and itself towards a book that appears to be an atlas. The four items are unforgettable now since you have created a series of links connecting all of them.

Location

Location is another important key to a productive memory. The map of memory is composed of locations. They serve as storage for mental filing, offering a natural and reliable way of preserving and recovering memories. This is due to the fact that we live in a three-dimensional universe whereby items could be found from where they exist or by applying a series of established coordinates, physically or mentally.

Location was initially applied as a memory device over 2,000 years ago. The old Greeks and eventually the Romans learned that forcing order on them was the perfect way of remembering things. They achieved this by picking a variety of places or locations they were already acquainted with. This might comprise of rooms, balconies, spires, portraits, and so on from around the building. Pictures of whatever they wished to remember would then be put at these different sites, or rather imagined.

Location restores order into our lives, and our lives will be in turmoil without it. Assume that you were told to write down, in sequence, all the things you did today. You will possibly begin by recreating your path, like me, and you would most probably apply the areas you have traveled through to serve as a guide.

We have previously described that it is likely to find a link among any two sets of data. Similarly, your brain will make a connection between any word, entity, opinion, or idea, and a location. Take the word "seven": it's simply a figure at first glimpse. However, once you enable your imagination to radiate easily, the word will lead you to a variety of related locations: the seventh heaven, the cottage of Snow White and the Seven Dwarves, the school you went through when you were seven, and so forth.

Location, therefore, is an important memory mastery building-block, since it lends itself well to connection. I apply it in a variety of my methods of memorization. It is the crucial part of the Journey Method

Imagination

Imagination is the power of memory. Imagination is not simply the ability to form a visual picture: it is the mind's maximum creative force. It is not simply a resource of authors, musicians, or writers, but a resource that we all have widely accessible.

Imagination is related to the Theta brainwave function, which is usually at its most effective mode when we dream. Nevertheless, at waking hours, small children, especially babies, generate a steady flow of this frequency, which may indicate the reason their imaginations sometimes run rampant. The boundaries between the actual and the imaginary are blurred since a teddy bear becomes a live friend and a robotic doll gains supernatural properties.

When we assume adulthood's roles and ambitions, the creativity that was once given free reign is reduced. I agree that the amount of stimuli an individual is provided as a kid and the level of resistance they display to fresh ideas in adulthood are directly associated.

You would train your imagination in a multitude of manners in this book, and the more you train it, the simpler it would be to create cognition-building images, views, and opinions and with ever-rising clarity and speed. If your imagination gets more vibrant, your mind will become stronger: all you need is to encourage it to come out and play.

The Journey Method

It is now the time to bring together the previous three memory keys, connection, place, and imagination, by combining them into what I think is the most effective and total memorization technique for any knowledge list. You will use all the strategies you have previously learned: association to be specific and the Link Method. I mainly developed this technique to break world records, and it was the key tool in enabling me to defeat my rivals. I name it the journey Method, and I think it will be crucial in transforming your memory to be more productive.

Begin by selecting a location you are acquainted with, such as your house, your office, your home county, or a park close by. The principle is to use this location to schedule a quick trip comprising of myriads of locations or stops along the way. The locations are then applied to mentally register the things you want to memorize on the list. The path you are taking will maintain the list's original order.

You would notice, like me, after a little while, that you do have a favorite trip which you may take to memorize nearly every sort of detail for daily use. In other words, when you have to use this strategy, you won't have to plan a new journey: you may just clean up your current favorite journey and use it again and again to preserve the new collection of knowledge you want to memorize.

Nevertheless, you would require more than one trip if you like to retain detail for long-term storage or various collections of information in the shorter term. For starters, I need several journeys while I am planning for record efforts or memory contests. I will send you examples of various routes in order for you to practice using various journeys. It equally helps when your selected location is important to the unique data you want to memorize. For instance, I may want to memorize sporting statistics during a journey to my local leisure centre.

Your home is perhaps the place you are most acquainted with. So let us use a typical house design to illustrate the way to memorize a quick list of 10 tasks for the day "to do." Choose a path via your personal home comprising of 10 stops.

Concentrations

We all have some days in which we find it hard to focus: we possibly feel under pressure or excessively exhausted. We are highly productive on some other days, ready, full of passion, and in balance. You've possibly heard the word "in the Zone," which is often used to explain the mental condition of high-performance sportsmen and women, for instance, whenever a tennis player annihilates his or her rival in a major tournament final. So what basically is this zone, and shouldn't we all have access to it?

We all emit a range of frequencies, varying from slow Delta waves, connected with relaxing, stress management, and rest, to quick Beta waves, connected with increased brain activity, judgment, and analytical thinking. All of these various frequencies have their unique purposes in our lives and serve some positive roles. y The development of Beta waves, for instance, helps us to handle the realistic, everyday side of life, though if we generated just these waves all the time, we might not have time to recover, dream or recall effectively.

The Practice of Revision and Optimizing Recall

We already looked at different strategies for memorizing a variety of information in this chapter, including simple shopping lists, directions, etc. The three elements of association, location, and imagination are involved in several of these strategies. Applying the Journey Method specifically, focused on familiar places, seems to fill the void between short- and long-term retention. It's as if the information bypasses the short-term memory, enabling more details to go right into the long-term memory storage. These memory strategies reduce the drudgery of conventional rote learning approaches, which in contrast can be sluggish, redundant, and less effective. Though it's important to understand the time and how often to revisit it to make sure the details stay in your long-term memory.

Ebbinghaus and The Curve of Recall

The German philosopher Hermann Ebbinghaus (1850–1909) was a part of the first individuals to conduct research on human memory. Using a sequence of random syllables, he invented a way to test memory, apparently pointless, unmemorable syllables, such as DAJ. He will read many times via a list of 20 such objects before committing the exact series to memory. After different periods, he, therefore, assessed his retention of the list. This was possibly the first structured learning curve ever made. Ebbinghaus found that it was simpler to remember details at the start and end of the list for a collection of details than for details in the middle. These patterns are referred to as Primacy and Recency's consequences, respectively, and a U-shaped graph graphically demonstrated the results.

Ebbinghaus equally found that the best way to preserve full recall was to constantly update information until what he termed "overlearning" had been accomplished. You have to understand the time to revisit it in order to strengthen the memory of the stored information.

How to Store a Memory in a Memory

Now we will use the real items from whatever list you want to commit to memory as the hooks to link to other things you want to recall: in other words, you will store a memory inside a memory.

Healthy Body, Productive Memory

You will be developing your memory throughout this book by focusing on your mind: pushing it to the extreme with a range of tough exercises and strategies. When you want to make changes in memory capacity, mental exercise is crucial, but the other component of you cannot be overlooked. In other words, you can optimize the benefits of your memory development by strengthening your body, as well.

Over time, I have learned that people who appear comfortable and extremely strong are the contestants that do especially well in memory contests. There are surely variations, but I can tell from practice that the best outcomes have appeared to follow a physical and also mental training period.

Our brains depend on oxygen, and I think daily physical activity is by far the most productive solution to support in transporting oxygen to the cells of the brain. I'm not saying this involves racing a half-marathon each month, but it's better than nothing for some sort of exercise which may gently increase your heart rate and cause you to feel mildly out of breath. Go for around thirty minutes daily to do some sort of physical exercise.

Nutrition equally plays a role in helping to preserve our memory in total working condition. It has been proven that foods high in antioxidant vitamins A, C, and E help the memory function productively. Such vitamins are abundant in richly colored fruit and veggies, like pineapple, cherry tomatoes, spinach, and citrus. They serve to clean up chemicals called free radicals that may lead to cell damage in the brain. Folic acid and other essential fatty acids (to be specific, omega-3 oils) are present in oily fish, like salmon, both of which are important for keeping a productive brain and nervous system. Dietary supplements, like Ginkgo Biloba, may help to move oxygen to the cells of the brain.

Stress and Stimulation

Several of the individuals that have received training do so in the illusion that memory strategies alone can resolve all their memory-related issues. Nevertheless, upon research, what seems to lie at the core of a decrease in their memory function is a large rise in stress in their lives. While you can empower these individuals to practice with the strategies outlined in this book on a regular basis, you can also help them recognize what could be the causes of their stress.

The human body releases massive quantities of adrenaline in stressful conditions. This is a basic method of survival regarded as the mechanism of "flight or fright." Nevertheless, this response is unnecessary in most stressful circumstances today, and thus the adrenaline is not consumed. It keeps building up in our bodies. Memory exposure to persistent or intense stress is severely harmful.

As a consequence of stress, the brain seizes to generate new neurons, but the resulting absence of mental stimulation will make existing neurons die. We have to find a perfect equilibrium between relaxing our minds and nurturing them, and shielding them from the dangers of stress.

Chapter 12:
Feedback And Iteration

Meaning of Feedback

Feedback is a mechanism in which learners make sense of their progress information and apply it to improve the quality of their work or techniques for learning. The word feedback is also applied to represent all sorts of remarks, including suggestions, praise, and appraisal, made after the fact. Although none of these is feedback, technically speaking.

Basically, feedback is data on the way we are doing in our attempts to accomplish an objective. You hit a tennis ball, and you watch where it lands with the intention of holding it on the court, in or out. You say a joke with the intention of causing people to laugh, and you watch the response of the audience as they laugh out loudly or barely snicker. You teach a lecture with the intention of facilitating learning, and you see that some learners have their eyes transfixed on you while others nod off.

Essentials of Feedback

Whether feedback is either there to be received or given by another person. Beneficial feedback is goal-oriented; tangible and transparent; actionable; user-friendly (specific and personalized); timely; ongoing; and reliable,

Goal-Oriented

Effective feedback implies that an entity has an objective, takes steps to achieve the goal, and provides details about his or her activities related to the goal. I said a joke to you... why? to get them to chuckle. I put up a story to involve the reader with vibrant language and realistic conversation that catches the emotions of the characters. I went up to the bat to get a hit. I do not get useful input if I am not sure about my priorities or if I refuse to pay attention to them (nor am I likely to reach my goals).

Data becomes feedback If, and only if, I attempt to trigger something and the data informs me whether I am on the course or have to change direction. I have to understand if some joke or part of my writing does not work, a revealing, nonconfrontational expression.

Notice that goals are always ambiguous in daily circumstances, although reasonably clear to all. When I say that joke, I don't have to declare that my intention is to cause you to laugh. But learners are often confused about the basic purpose of a task or lesson in school, so it is important to remind them of the aim and the standards against which they can judge themselves. A teacher might say, for instance,

The purpose of this writing assignment is for you to trigger your readers to laugh. So, anytime you go over your draft or get peer reviews, inquire how humorous the draft is? Where may the funniest thing be?

When preparing a table poster to demonstrate the results of your science experiment, note that the goal is to engage individuals in your project as well as to explain the facts that you have learned during your study. Self-evaluate the role using these rubrics against those two parameters. The science fair judges will do the same.

Tangible and Transparent

Every effective feedback system encompasses not only a specific target but also concrete outcomes relevant to the purpose. Individuals laugh, giggle, or not laughing at the joke; students are extremely attentive, very attentive, or inattentive to my teaching.

We are learning from such tangible input even as little children. That's the way we learn to talk; to grip a spoon; and to know that certain words mysteriously generate food, drink, or a change of clothes from great people. The best input is so tangible that someone who has an objective will benefit from it.

Alas, as described in a real story an educator told me years ago, educational feedback is opaque. "At the end of the year, a classmate went straight to her and said, "Miss Jones, all year long you continued writing this same phrase on my English papers, and I really don't understand what it implies." "What's the exact expression?" she asked. "Vag-oo," he responded. (The term that was vague!)

Often the performers don't understand it, even though the knowledge is tangible and clear, either because they don't search for it or as they are too occupied trying to concentrate on the impact. In sports, inexperienced tennis players or batters frequently do not know they are taking their eyes off the ball; whenever the feedback is provided, they often protest. (Shouting loudly, "Keep your eye on the ball!" seldom works.) And we've all noticed how often new teachers are so busy focusing on "teaching" that they don't care that few students are listening or learning.

That's the reason video or audio recordings could enable us to discern items which we may not recognize as we practice, in addition to input from coaches or other able analysts; and by implication, such recordings help us learn to search for knowledge that is difficult to perceive but vital. I suggest that all teachers at least once a month videotape their own lessons. When I did it as a starting coach, it was a powerful experience for me. As I was teaching, ideas that were crystal clear to me seemed opaque and downright confusing on tape, even caught in the many quizzical looks of my students that I had overlooked at the moment.

Actionable

Successful input is concrete, specific and helpful; it offers knowledge that is actionable. "Good job!" and "You did that wrong," and B+ is also not suggestions at all. In reaction to these comments, we can easily envision the learners questioning themselves, What else should I explicitly do more or less next time, based on this information? Uh, no idea. They have no idea what is "good" or "wrong" in what they have done.

Actionable input must be acknowledged by the artist as well. Many so-called feedback situations lead to complaints because the donors are not informative enough; instead of merely presenting the data, they leap to a conclusion from the data. For instance, a supervisor may make the terrible but normal mistake of saying that "many students were bored in class." That is a judgement, not an observation. It would have been much more beneficial and less debatable if the supervisor had said something like, "I observed ongoing unobservant habits in 12 of the 25 students once the lecture was ongoing. The habits comprised messaging under desks, exchanging glances, and engaging in conversation with other students. Nevertheless, after the small-group exercise started, I saw such conduct in just one student."

More broadly, such caution in presenting neutral, goal-related information is the whole point of clinical supervision of teaching and good coaching. Based on a simple statement of priorities, successful managers and coaches strive diligently to examine and reflect on what they have learned closely. That's why I always inquire, "What do you want me to look for and perhaps count?" I have always found such pure input to be acknowledged and appreciated in my experience as an instructor. Successful coaches often recognize that actionable feedback about what went right is as valuable as feedback about what did not work in dynamic performance situations.

User-Friendly

Even when feedback is precise and reliable in the eyes of professionals or observers, it is not of much importance if the consumer does not comprehend it or is confused by it. For a beginner, highly technical input will appear strange and confusing. It is doubtful that explaining a baseball strike to a 6-year-old in terms of momentum and other physics ideas would create a better hitter. Too much feedback is also unhelpful; it is easier to help the participant focus on either one or two main performance indicators than to generate a buzz of data from all sides.

Specialist coaches regularly avoid bombarding participants with too much or too much technological details. They tell the participants that one significant thing they found is that if modified, rapid and visible changes will likely be made ("I was baffled about who was talking in the conversation you wrote in this paragraph"). They do not give advice until they make sure that the artist knows the meaning of what they have seen.

Timely

In most instances, the faster I obtain input, the better. For hours or days, I wouldn't want to try to find out if my students were responsive and if they knew, or what part of my written story works and which part doesn't. To make circumstances such as playing a piano piece in a recital, I say "in most cases." When I act, I don't like my instructor or the audience shouting out suggestions. That's why it is more accurate suggesting that good feedback is "timely" instead of "immediate.".

Ill-timed feedback, nevertheless, is a major problem in education. Days, weeks, or even months after success, critical feedback on main outcomes often comes from writing and handing in papers or bringing back reports on test scores. As teachers, we should work overtime and find methods to ensure that learners receive more timely input and incentives to use it when their minds are still fresh from the attempt and effects.

Remember that input does not have to come only from the teacher, or even from people at all before you think this is impossible. Technology is a powerful instrument, and unrestricted, timely input and opportunities to use it are part of the power of computer-assisted learning. Another technique for handling the load is peer review to ensure a lot of timely feedback; nevertheless, it is necessary to teach people to do high-standard small-group peer review without inappropriate critique or unconstructive praise.

Continuation

Adjusting our success relies not only on getting feedback but also on having the chance to use it. What renders every educational appraisal formative is not simply that it precedes summative evaluations, but that if outcomes are less than satisfactory, the performer has opportunities to transform the output to better reach the objective. The feedback arrives too late in summative evaluation; the result is done.

Therefore, the more real-time feedback I can get, the better my overall success will be. This is how all video games that are really popular work. You understand that the secret to significant change is that the feedback is both timely and continuous whether you play Angry Birds, Halo, Guitar Hero, or Tetris. If you lose, you should start over again, or even right where you left off, and get another chance to gain feedback and learn from it. (This effective feedback loop is also user-friendly. Games are intended to reflect and adjust to our evolving information processing needs, speed, and capacity.)

It is telling, too, that performers are frequently evaluated in view of feedback on their capacity to adjust. In a wide variety of ways, the ability to quickly change one's success is a mark of all great accomplishments and problem solvers. Or, as many minor league coaches claim, "The issue is not making mistakes; you will all lose several balls in the field, and that's part of the learning process. The issue would be when you don't grow from the mistakes."

Strategies To Provide Productive Feedback

- In nature, feedback should be educative.

Providing reviews implies providing students with an interpretation of what they are doing right and wrong. However, the emphasis of the feedback should basically be focused on what the students are doing correctly. When a description and illustration are given as to what is true and incorrect about their job, it is most productive for a student's learning.

To direct your feedback, consider trying the idea of a 'feedback sandwich': compliment, right, a compliment.

- Feedback should be offered in a timely manner

The student reacts positively whenever feedback is offered immediately after demonstrating signs of learning and recognizes the understanding of what is being learned in a confident way. The moment is wasted when we wait too long to provide feedback, and the student does not associate the feedback with the action.

- Be attentive to the student's personal requirements.

When providing feedback, it is important that we take every student individually into account. Our classrooms are full of students who are diverse. In order to succeed at a higher level, many students have to be nudged, and others have to be treated very kindly so as not to discourage learning and harm self-esteem. It is important to provide a balance between not wanting to damage a student's feelings and offering sufficient encouragement.

- Ask these four questions.

Studies of effective teaching and learning have also revealed that learners like to recognize where they stand in terms of their job. Supplying responses on a routine basis to the following four questions would better offer quality feedback. When providing parents with input, these four questions are also useful:

What would a student do about it?

What can't the student do?

How does the work of a student compare to that of others?

How is a student able to do better?

- Feedback should refer to ability or unique expertise

When rubrics become a helpful method, this is (single-point rubrics, for example). A rubric is a means to articulate expectations for an assignment and a valuable way to provide effective learning input. In contrast with an existing set of criteria, successful rubrics provide students with very precise details about their results. Try highlighting rubric elements that the student is meeting for younger learners or using a sticker map.

- Offer feedback to hold students 'on track' for accomplishment.

Daily 'check-ins' with students will let them know where they are and with you in the classroom—using the '4 questions' to direct your reviews.

- Conduct a one-on-one conference.

One of the most productive means of providing input is to have a one-on-one meeting with a student. The student will be looking forward to the attention and will be eager to ask the required questions. Broadly speaking, a one-on-one meeting should be constructive, as this will allow the student to look forward to the next meeting.

This technique, as with all aspects of teaching, involves effective time management. While the other students are working independently, try meeting with a student. Time the meetings in order not to last more than 10 minutes.

- You may provide input verbally, non-verbally, or in written form.

Make sure your frowns are kept in place. It is important that we analyze our non-verbal signals. Facial expressions and movements are also forms of input transmission. This implies that it is best not to scowl when you hand back that English document.

- Focus on one skill or ability.

Where only one talent is questioned, it has a much stronger effect on the student, opposed to the whole paper being the subject of all that is incorrect.

- Alternate due dates for your classes/students.

To provide effective support for learning, use this technique while grading papers or exams. This approach gives you the time required for quality, written input to be given. This can also involve using a rotation chart at a deeper, more practical level for students to confer with. Students will also realize when it's their turn to see you and are more likely to bring their own questions to the meeting.

- Teach students how to give one another feedback.

A model of what suitable input looks and sounds like to students. We call this 'peer conferencing' as an elementary teacher. Prepare the students to provide meaningful input to each other in a supportive and beneficial way. Encourage students to record the given feedback using post-it notes.

- Request another adult to provide feedback.

At the college I taught, the director would occasionally volunteer to grade history exams or read pieces of writing by students. You can imagine how tenfold the standard of the student's work improved! Invite a 'guest' instructor or student teacher to criticize work if the principal is too busy (and most are),

- Have the students make notes.

The student will do the writing as you do the talking during a conference about a test, paper, or a general 'check-in.' The student should jot down notes using a notebook while you provide verbal input.

- Use a diary to keep track of student advances.

For every student, hold a portion of a journal. Write daily or weekly, dated comments as needed about each student. Keep records of the student's excellent questions, disciplinary problems, areas for change, test scores, etc. This requires a lot of important time management, of course, so when it's time for a student or parent to talk, you're ready to go.

- At the start of class, return exam papers, test papers, or comment cards.

Learning By Iteration

One way of improving an ability is to make it a pattern stored in the structure of the students. The most critical first step in making this possible is to carry the capacity to a cognitive awareness where the student intentionally cares about the practice (not necessarily the skill).

In other words, the student realizes what ability they need and works on performing things that will help them improve that ability. This can be termed as learning by iteration.

The task becomes simpler and easier when a skill is exercised or practiced over days and weeks, thus inherently pushing the ability to a psychological level where it is indefinitely preserved at any moment for recollection and repetitive use.

The student no longer has to actively worry about their engagement in the ability-building activity until the ability improves. Similarly, it is obvious that new skills have been developed when a new task becomes very simple.

The skill training must be administered over several days each week and over at least a three-month span to establish ample closely related iterations that push a newly reinforced skill into a subconscious, autopilot mode.

For instance, the more efforts a child makes when learning the way to ride a bike, the better the brain emphasizes the basic skills required to remain stable and in action. After some period, to remain upright, stable, and in motion, or how to stop without falling off, the kid doesn't need to stop and ponder about each part of the operation. The ability is strengthened each time the child drives. Many years later, since it was so deeply embedded in the brain, it is possible for an individual to get on a bike and ride without extra riding experience. This is the strength of learning through iteration.

How to Use Iteration for Learning

It is one thing to have a plan, but then it's a matter of applying it and keeping details. Also, if a plan is too complex for you, it is simple to get into this 4-step technique and should produce similar results.

- Revise Your notes

Inside 20-24 hours of the first intake of details, ensure the details are written down on paper and that you have checked them for short-term storage. Over the revising phase, you like to read them but then turn away and try to remember the most significant ideas.

Note, there is a distinction between rereading and remembering, so make sure you turn away from your away and pull from your memory.

- Remember the Details for the First Time

Try retrieving the details after some hours or a day without looking at any of your notes as often. When you take a stroll or sit down and relax, try to remember it.

By making postcards of the central concepts and challenging yourself on the concepts, you can also improve your productivity.

- Recall the material again

After that, retrieve the content every 24-36 hours over the period of several days. They need not be long study periods. Whenever you're sitting on a chair or standing in line, try a recall session. You are always free to look at your notes or postcards. However, try to remember as you work with those notes. With this step, the aim is to raise questions and challenge yourself in order to keep this knowledge in your long-term memory and remember it.

- Study it all over again

Bring out your content after many days have passed and reviewed it all over again. Make sure that this is completed within a week before the exam if this knowledge is for a test. It helps the brain to reprocess theories.

Conclusion

Learning is as unpredictable a thing to understand as camphor. You should not place a restriction on your capacity to learn simply to manage it according to your desires. What we've learned in this book gives us a different perspective. We discovered that our memory and ability to learn are limitless and can be improved beyond measure. So, we should try to tame it in order to make it our slave.

The guidelines, tactics, and strategies published in this book are proven approaches, tried and tested by many like you. Learning difficulties are prevalent, more so among learners. Most cases of an inability to learn effectively worsen academic outcomes. This book demonstrated and clarified how memory could be sharpened and transformed into a sophisticated tool for limitless learning. It discusses topics that are commonly overlooked when it comes to providing support with a poor memory.

Creativity and concentration are the solutions to a lot of problems, and one of them is the memory crisis. Note, you are using just ten percent of the memory in your brain. Ninety percent of the remainder are all inactive memories lying around. If you manage to update even five percent of the ten open, you have effectively mastered your memory. The chapters provided various approaches to accelerate your learning ability, including lifestyle and reading, two frequently overlooked elements of learning.

In order to attain a productive state in learning, a balance should be struck between the difficulty of the learning task and the learner's potential. Learning flow does not happen if the assignment is too easy or too hard. It is important to balance and match both skill level and difficulty level; if skill and difficulty are low and balanced, then it leads to apathy, anxiety, or concern. The better we can evaluate and appreciate every individual's distinctive styles and learning preferences, the more we can tailor learning, accommodate for complex team differences, and maximize the experience of flow.

Thanks for buying this book. I hope you enjoyed reading it and that it was enjoyable as well as insightful.

References

- Bracey, R. (2018). *Boost Your IQ Tips and Techniques for a Sharper Mind.* Erscheinungsort nicht ermittelbar: Watkins Media.
- Bransford, J. D. (2004). *How people learn: Brain, mind, experience, and school.* Washington, DC: National Acad. Press.
- Carey, B. (2015). *How we learn: The surprising truth about when, where, and why it happens.* New York, NY: Random House.
- Craig, D., & Kohl, K. (2014). *Accelerated learning for breakthrough results: Whole brain, person and system approach to accelerated learning, engagement, change and growth.* Randburg, South Africa: Knowres Publishing.
- Hollins, P. (2017). *The science of accelerated learning: Advances strategies for quicker comprehension, greater retention, and systematic expertise.* CreateSpace Independent Publishing Platform.
- Howie, D. D. (1997). *NLP: Advanced psychological skills for the thinking manager.* England: Rushmere Wynne.

- Mccullough, J. (2014). *Accelerated learning techniques for students: Learn more in less time*. North Charleston, SC: CreateSpace Independent Publishing Platform.
- Rose, C. P., & Nicholl, M. J. (2002). *Accelerated learning for the 21st century = Cara belajar cepat abad XXI*. Bandung: Nuansa.
- Schwartz, E. M. (1965). *How to double your power to learn*.
- Segler, H. (2015). *Learning: How to become a genius and expert in any subject with accelerated learning*. Charleston, SC: Createspace Independent Publishing Platform.
- Smith, A. (2005). *Accelerated Learning in Practice: Brain-based methods for accelerating motivation and achievembrain-based methods for accelerated learning*. Oxford: Network Education Press.
- Thomas, D. (2003). *Improving your memory*. New York: DK Pub.
- Vaughn, D. E. (2007). *How to remember anything: The proven total memory retention system*. New York: St. Martin's Griffin.
- Wainwright, G. R., & Wainwright, G. R. (2010). *How to speed read*. Oxford: How To Books.

- Weinland, J. D. (1986). *How to improve your memory.* New York: Harper & Row.
- Willink, T. (2019). *Accelerated learning: A beginner's guide to learn faster and better without stress, worry and anxiety by unlocking your brain's unlimited memory.*
- Willis, J. (2015). *How Your Child Learns Best Brain-Friendly Strategies You Can Use to Ignite Your Child's Learning and Increase School Success.* Sourcebooks.

www.ingramcontent.com/pod-product-compliance
Lightning Source LLC
Chambersburg PA
CBHW021437080526
44588CB00009B/573